Fresh Ways with
Beef and Veal

COVER
A veal escalope is wrapped round a light stuffing of gingered cranberries. After it is cooked, the stuffed veal olive is sliced, revealing the contrasting interior, and then sauced with the seasoned fruit juice in which it was braised (recipe, page 100).

TIME-LIFE BOOKS

EUROPEAN EDITOR: Ellen Phillips
Design Director: Ed Skyner
Director of Editorial Resources: Louise Tulip
Chief Sub-Editor: Ilse Gray

HEALTHY HOME COOKING

SERIES DIRECTOR: Dale M. Brown
Series Administrator: Elise Ritter Gibson
Designer (acting): Elissa E. Baldwin
Picture Editor: Sally Collins
Text Editor: Allan Fallow
Editorial Assistant: Rebecca C. Christofferson

Editorial Staff for *Fresh Ways with Beef and Veal:*
Book Manager: Susan Stuck
Designer: Lynne Brown
Associate Picture Editor: Scarlet Cheng
Researcher/Writers: Henry Grossi, Andrea Reynolds
Sub-Editors: Wendy Gibbons, Elizabeth Graham, Ruth Baja Williams
Picture Co-ordinator: Linda Yates
Photographer's Assistant: Mazya Parvaresh
Kitchen Assistant: Chhomaly Sok

Editorial Production:
Production Chief: Maureen Kelly
Assistant: Deborah Fulham
Editorial Department: Theresa John, Debra Lelliott

THE COOKS

PAT ALBUREY is a home economist with a wide experience of preparing foods for photography, teaching cookery and creating recipes. She has contributed to a number of cookery books and was the studio consultant for the Time-Life Series *The Good Cook.*

LISA CHERKASKY has worked as a chef in Madison, Wisconsin, and in Washington, D.C. She is a graduate of the Culinary Institute of America.

ADAM DE VITO began his cooking apprenticeship when he was only 14. He has worked at Le Pavillon restaurant in Washington, D.C., taught with cookery author Madeleine Kamman, and conducted classes at L'Académie de Cuisine.

JOHN T. SHAFFER is a graduate of The Culinary Institute of America. He has had broad experience as a chef, including five years at the Four Seasons Hotel in Washington, D.C.

CONSULTANTS

CAROL CUTLER is the author of many cookery books. During the 12 years she lived in France, she studied at the Cordon Bleu and the École des Trois Gourmandes, as well as with private chefs.

NORMA MACMILLAN has written several cookery books and edited many others. She has worked on various cookery publications, including *Grand Diplôme* and *Supercook* and some of the recipes for this volume were created by her. She lives and works in London.

MARY JO FEENEY, who has a Master's degree in nutrition from Case-Western Reserve University, Cleveland, Ohio, is a registered dietician with 15 years experience in the health-care field. She is the author of the U.S. consumer information brochure *Light Cooking with Beef* and *California Beef*, a computerized cookery book.

NUTRITION CONSULTANTS

JANET TENNEY has been involved in nutrition and consumer affairs since she received her master's degree in human nutrition from Columbia University.

PATRICIA JUDD trained as a dietician and worked in hospital practice before returning to university to obtain her MSc and PhD degrees. Since then she has lectured in Nutrition and Dietetics at London University.

Nutritional analyses for *Fresh Ways with Beef and Veal* were derived from Practorcare's Nutriplanner System and other current data.

This volume is one of a series of illustrated cookery books that emphasize the preparation of healthy dishes for today's weight-conscious, nutrition-minded eaters.

▲

Fresh Ways with Beef and Veal

BY

THE EDITORS OF TIME-LIFE BOOKS

TIME-LIFE BOOKS/AMSTERDAM

Contents

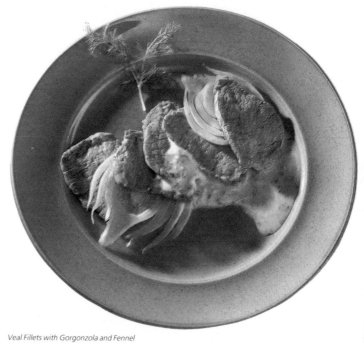

Barbecued Steaks with Shallots and Mushrooms

Barbecued Beef Stuffed with Summer Vegetables

Veal Fillets with Gorgonzola and Fennel

Veal, Peach and Peppercorn Pâté

4 A Medley of Ideas 109

5 Microwaving Beef and Veal 127

3 Moist and Gentle Cooking 81

Lime-Ginger Beef

The New, Lean Beef and Veal

Mention red meat and beef springs to mind, setting mouths to watering with the thought of majestic cuts and mighty flavour. So different is the pale flesh and subtle flavour of veal that it scarcely seems possible that these two meats come from the same animal.

What beef and veal share is the real satisfaction that they can offer to diner and cook alike. Both meats lend themselves to a variety of different cooking methods and unite happily with a wide range of other foods. Little wonder, then, that beef and veal have long occupied a place at the heart of the European culinary tradition.

This volume celebrates the old-fashioned virtues of beef and veal; but it does so in a modern way, concentrating on lean cuts cooked in little additional fat and served up in healthy 90 g (3 oz) portions (each based on 125 g/4 oz of trimmed raw meat). The recipes thus make it possible for lovers of beef and veal to have their meat and address their health concerns too.

(3 oz) helpings of cooked, lean beef — which have less than 180 calories — supply 45 per cent of the 60 grams of protein that an adult should have in his or her daily diet. Beef also contains many of the nutrients that we need in minute amounts —milligrams or micrograms — in our diet. A 90 g (3 oz) portion of cooked beef supplies all of the vitamin B12, about 20 per cent of the niacin and about 30 per cent of the thiamine an adult male should consume daily. The same portion also provides 25 per cent of his daily iron requirement.

Moreover, 40 to 60 per cent of the iron in beef is present as part of the haemoglobin molecule, which gives blood its red colour. Since this so-called "haem iron" is readily absorbed by the body, beef has particular importance to women, for whom iron ranks high among the essential minerals. Haem iron is also valuable for its ability to enhance the body's absorption of iron from other foods.

Veal has even fewer calories — a mere 120 calories being present in a 100 g (3½ oz) escalope.

In developing the 109 dishes that follow, the Time-Life cooks have heeded recommendations from nutritionists that we cut down on the fat in our diet. Studies have shown that we obtain some 40 per cent of our calories from fat and that we would be much better off if we reduced that amount to around 30 per cent. As the recipes in this volume will demonstrate, this is a goal that can be met by wisely selecting and preparing lean cuts of beef and veal, without compromising taste or curtailing the pleasure both meats so abundantly offer. The cooks have been particularly careful to restrict the amount of saturated fat in their recipes, since it is this fat that raises the level of cholesterol in the blood and increases the risk of heart disease. Nutritionists recommend that less than 15 per cent of our calories should come from saturated fat.

And, with today's trend towards lean, super-trimmed cuts, veal can have a fat level as low as 5 per cent.

Contrary to what most people believe, beef and veal are not overloaded with cholesterol. A 100 g (3½ oz) serving of beef, for example, averages 85 milligrams of cholesterol, the same weight of veal 90 milligrams of cholesterol. Most other meats and some fish have cholesterol levels comparable with beef and veal.

For our dishes, we have chosen beef and veal cuts *(diagrams, page 9)* from the least fatty parts of the animals. Yet it is fat, of course, that gives meat, especially red meat, much of its flavour and juiciness. Because we have avoided the fattier cuts, we have employed methods and ingredients that ensure flavour and moistness. And we have been very careful not to overcook the meat — which is easy to do with lean cuts, particularly when pieces are small. Prolonged high heat is the surest way to toughen meat, and to dry it out and shrink it as well.

The nutritional aspects

Beef and veal are very good for you. They are considered nutrient-dense foods, which means, simply, that they provide a high level of essential nutrients with relatively few calories. This book's 90 g

For roasting, grilling and barbecuing beef we recommend that it be cooked rare or medium rare. In large cuts this can be ascertained by inserting a meat thermometer into the thickest part of the meat and letting the temperature reach 60°C (140°F). (Such a temperature also guarantees that any harmful organisms which might be present will be killed.) An instant-reading thermometer, which registers temperatures just 10 seconds after insertion, can be very handy, especially when the piece is small. After the desired 60°C (140°F) temperature has been reached, let the beef rest away from the heat for up to 15 minutes, during which time its internal temperature will rise five more degrees — just right for medium-rare beef. Veal, however, is most palatable when its juices have lost their pink tinge; like beef, it becomes tough when overcooked.

Because the recipes call for very small amounts of cooking oil, we encourage the use of non-stick frying pans wherever possible. To further keep down calories and to restrict saturated fat, we make little use of cream, butter and cheese in sauces. Any fat that may have melted out of the meat is discarded. We obtain smooth, well-flavoured sauces by reducing the liquids in which the meat and other ingredients have been simmered, thus retaining their nutrients.

With tougher cuts, we may pound the meat to tenderize it. By carving diagonally across the grain, we produce slices that are easy to chew. Sometimes, we cut meat into small pieces or strips so that they can cook quickly. For stir-frying, the raw meat is sliced into thin strips and tossed in a wok or frying pan, then removed and replaced by the vegetables called for in the dish. Only when the vegetables are ready is the meat returned to the pan and reheated, a measure that keeps it from overcooking and turning leathery. We do not salt the meat before grilling, roasting or barbecuing it because salt draws out the juices, producing dry meat.

Reshaping the animals themselves

Thanks to the meat industry's efforts, beef and veal are leaner than they used to be. Farmers are raising leaner beef breeds, such as Limousin and Charolais. Cattle spend more time eating grass and less time being finished, or fattened, on grain than in the past. Many veal calves are now reared in barns and allowed to move freely. This arrangement is not only more humane than the old system of keeping the calves in confined spaces; it also burns up energy and results in a leaner carcass.

As farmers strive for leaner cattle, so retailers aim for leaner cuts, often employing a seam-butchery technique that removes muscle and bone, and trims fat to within 3 mm (1/8 inch) of the flesh. You should buy trimmed meat and further trim it at home.

Storing beef and veal

Both meats are less perishable than poultry and fish. Steaks and larger cuts can be kept for up to four days in a refrigerator set between 2°C (35°F) and 6°C (43°F). Minced meat should never be kept longer than two to three days. For storage, meat from the butcher should be unwrapped, set on a plate, loosely covered with wax paper, then covered with a dish that allows air to circulate, thus eliminating the damp environment that causes bacteria to thrive. Cuts from the supermarket sold in special airtight wrapping can be stored in their wrapping.

Preparing meat for freezing involves wrapping it tightly in tough moisture and vapour-proof plastic, aluminium foil or freezer paper, then squeezing all air from the package. Air pockets cause freezer burn, which dries out meat and alters its colour, texture and flavour.

Properly wrapped joints or pieces of beef may be kept in a freezer for up to a year and veal for six months, providing they are quickly frozen and maintained at −18°C (0°F) or lower. Any meat, whether beef or veal, that has been minced should not be kept longer than six months.

About the book's organization

This book falls into five sections, covering respectively roasting and grilling, stir-fries and sautés, moist methods, mixed methods and a final microwave chapter. In each section, the beef recipes are grouped together, followed by the veal recipes. Most recipes come with suggestions for accompanying vegetables or starches. For generalized techniques common to a number of the recipes, such as stuffing a steak or rolling a paupiette of veal, there are step-by-step instructions.

Dry-heat methods such as grilling and stir-frying are generally applied to tender roasts and chops. Moist-heat methods such as braising are reserved mostly for tougher cuts. Vegetables are often cooked with the meat to provide moisture as well as flavour and herbs, and spices, fruits and fruit juices, wines and spirits are called upon to increase the savour of the dishes, all of which are low in salt. Many of the recipes ask for unsalted brown, veal or chicken stock *(recipes, page 138)*. A glossary towards the end of the volume identifies and describes ingredients or techniques that may be unfamiliar.

With every recipe, metric and imperial weights are given for each ingredient and, although close equivalents, the two systems should not be mixed for the same recipe. All recipes not only take into account your concerns about fat but also provide information about nutrition in general. Printed beside each recipe is a breakdown of nutrients per single serving — approximate counts for calories, protein, cholesterol, total fat, saturated fat (the kind that increases the body's blood cholesterol) and sodium. This analysis should make it easier for you to plan the rest of your meal — and the other menus for the day as well — so that you can ensure that fewer of the calories you consume come from fat.

The Key to Better Eating

Healthy Home Cooking addresses the concerns of today's weight-conscious, health-minded cooks with recipes developed within strict nutritional guidelines.

The chart (right) gives dietary guidelines for healthy men, women and children. Recommended figures vary from country to country, but the principles are the same everywhere. Here, the average daily amounts of calories and protein are from a report by the U.K. Department of Health and Social Security; the maximum advisable daily intake of fat is based on guidelines given by the National Advisory Committee on Nutrition Education (NACNE); those for cholesterol and sodium are based on upper limits suggested by the World Health Organization.

The volumes in the Healthy Home Cooking series do not purport to be diet books, nor do they focus on health foods. Rather, the books express a commonsense approach to cooking that uses salt, sugar, cream, butter and oil in moderation while including other ingredients that also contribute flavour and satisfaction. The portions themselves are modest in size.

The recipes make few unusual demands. Naturally they call for fresh ingredients, offering substitutes should these be unavailable. (Only the original ingredient is calculated in the nutrient analysis, however.) Most of the in-

Recommended Dietary Guidelines

		Average Daily Intake		Maximum Daily Intake			
		CALORIES	PROTEIN grams	CHOLESTEROL milligrams	TOTAL FAT grams	SATURATED FAT grams	SODIUM milligrams
Females	7-8	1900	47	300	80	32	2000*
	9-11	2050	51	300	77	35	2000
	12-17	2150	53	300	81	36	2000
	18-54	2150	54	300	81	36	2000
	54-74	1900	47	300	72	32	2000
Males	7-8	1980	49	300	80	33	2000
	9-11	2280	57	300	77	38	2000
	12-14	2640	66	300	99	44	2000
	15-17	2880	72	300	108	48	2000
	18-34	2900	72	300	109	48	2000
	35-64	2750	69	300	104	35	2000
	65-74	2400	60	300	91	40	2000

*(or 5g salt)

gredients can be found in any well-stocked supermarket; the occasional exceptions can be bought in speciality or ethnic food shops.

About cooking times

To help the cook plan ahead effectively, Healthy Home Cooking takes time into account in all its recipes. While recognizing that everyone cooks at a different speed, and that stoves and ovens may differ somewhat in their temperatures, the series provides approximate "working" and "total" times

for every dish. Working time stands for the minutes actively spent on preparation; total time includes unattended cooking time, as well as time devoted to marinating, steeping or soaking various ingredients. Because the recipes emphasize fresh foods, the dishes may take a bit longer to prepare than those in "quick and easy" cookery books that call for canned or packaged products, but the difference in flavour, and often in added nutritional value, should compensate for the little extra time involved.

Chili Peppers — a Cautionary Note

Both dried and fresh hot chili peppers should be handled with care. Their flesh and seeds contain volatile oils that can make skin tingle and cause eyes to burn. Rubber gloves offer protection — but the cook should still be careful not to touch the face, lips or eyes when working with chili peppers.

Soaking fresh chili peppers in cold, salted water for an hour will remove some of their fire. If canned chilies are substituted for fresh ones, they should be rinsed in cold water in order to eliminate as much of the brine used to preserve them as possible.

The Leanest of the Lean

These diagrams show and identify the beef and veal cuts *(coloured areas)* that are used in the book. No cut derives more than 45 per cent of its calories from fat, and many come in well under that amount.

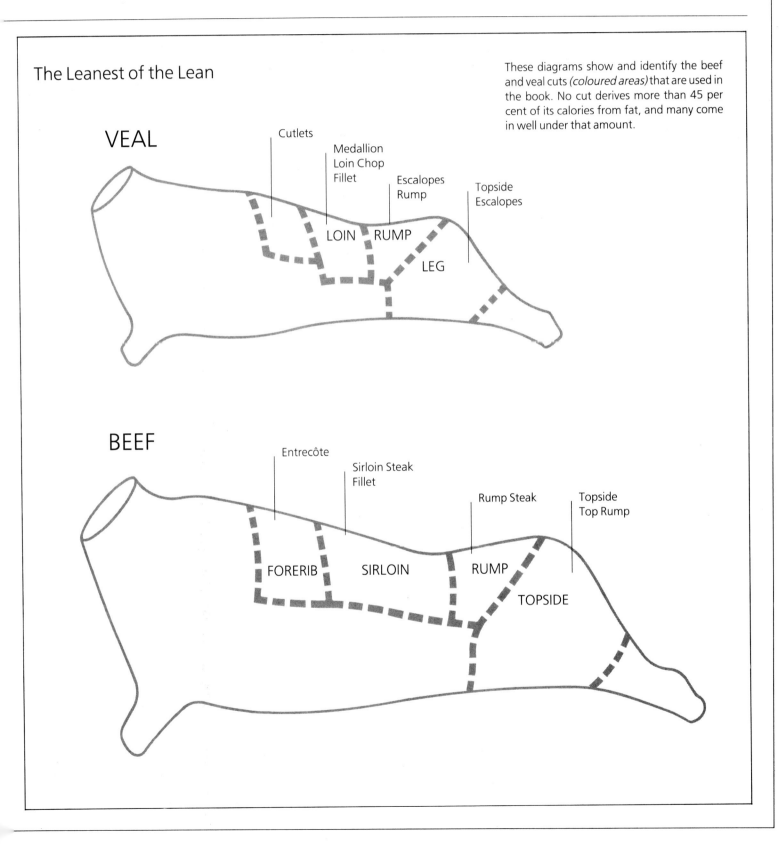

VEAL

Cutlets

Medallion
Loin Chop
Fillet

Escalopes
Rump

Topside
Escalopes

LOIN   RUMP

LEG

BEEF

Entrecôte

Sirloin Steak
Fillet

Rump Steak

Topside
Top Rump

FORERIB   SIRLOIN   RUMP

TOPSIDE

1 Spread with an aromatic blend of garlic, herbs and mustard, a lean, boned loin of veal lies ready to be trussed and roasted (recipe, page 54).

Techniques for Tender Cuts

The first cuts of beef and veal ever to be cooked were probably suspended over an open fire. Present-day roasting and grilling have much in common with that ancient technique in that they involve direct dry heat. Roasting employs the all-round heat of a modern oven, whereas grilling directs heat to only one side of the food at a time — either from above or from below. When beef and veal are subjected to this dry, potentially scorching heat, the chief concern of the cook is to prevent the flesh from drying out. The solution adopted by previous generations of cooks was fat in its many guises. Marbling in the muscle itself kept meat moist, as did lardons of pork fat threaded into the meat, bards of fat tied round it, and oil and butter smeared liberally over the joint and used to baste it.

Today, however, the health-conscious are concerned to cut down on fat in all its forms. Marbling varies from cut to cut, and this chapter has rejected fatty back-rib and forerib cuts which used to rank among the most popular joints for roasting. Instead, we have generally selected beef sirloin or rump, and veal fillet or loin. Minced beef is taken from a topside cut, and trimmed free of visible fat before being minced.

Fat for larding, barding and basting has also been drastically reduced. To compensate for lack of added fat, vegetable stuffings are often used here to baste beef from within by gradually releasing their natural moisture during cooking.

In the barbecued beef stuffed with summer vegetables *(page 24)*, for example, a stuffing of sweet green and red peppers combined with courgettes contributes moisture as well as flavour and colour. Again, on page 37, watercress, spinach and walnuts form a pinwheel pattern inside pink roulades of rare beef. When plain roast beef is the order of the day, a modern roasting bag provides one solution, protecting a sirloin from intense oven heat, while saving diners from unwanted calories *(page 39)*.

The lean delicate flesh of veal is saved from drying out by the imaginative use of oil-free marinades and coatings, all of them reflecting veal's ability to merge with a diverse range of flavourings. For example, in veal and apricot brochettes tikka-style *(page 36)*, a marinade that includes yogurt, ginger, lime and a catalogue of spices both succours the meat and flavours it. On a distinctly pungent note, a paste of green and black peppercorns provides a protective coat for veal fillet *(page 55)*. And on page 54, a boned loin of veal receives masterly low-calorie treatment — flavourings of grapefruit and herbs, and frequent bastings with stock.

Grilled Sirloin Steak with Peach Piccalilli

Serves 6
Working time: about 20 minutes
Total time: about 45 minutes

Calories **205**
Protein **24g**
Cholesterol **65mg**
Total fat **7g**
Saturated fat **3g**
Sodium **185mg**

850 g	sirloin steak in one piece, about 2.5 cm (1 inch) thick, trimmed of fat	1¾ lb
2 tsp	chopped fresh ginger root	2 tsp
⅛ tsp	cayenne pepper	⅛ tsp
¼ tsp	salt	¼ tsp
Peach piccalilli		
250 g	white onion	8 oz
350 g	ripe peaches	12 oz
½ tbsp	safflower oil	½ tbsp
1 tsp	chopped fresh ginger root	1 tsp
⅛ tsp	cayenne pepper	⅛ tsp
3 tbsp	red wine vinegar	3 tbsp
⅛ tsp	salt	⅛ tsp
4 tbsp	fresh orange juice	4 tbsp
1½ tbsp	chopped fresh coriander or parsley	1½ tbsp

To start the piccalilli, slice the onions in half lengthwise. Cutting with the grain, slice each half into strips about 5 mm (¼ inch) wide. Blanch the peaches in boiling water for 30 seconds, then remove them with a slotted spoon. When the peaches are cool enough to handle, peel and stone them; cut the peaches into thin slices.

Heat the oil in a large, non-stick frying pan over medium-low heat. Add the onion, ginger and cayenne pepper and cook the onion until it is translucent — 7 to 10 minutes. Stir in the vinegar and salt, then cook the mixture for 1 minute more. Add the peaches and orange juice. Cook the piccalilli slowly, until the peaches are soft but not mushy — an additional 12 to 15 minutes. Remove the pan from the heat and stir in the coriander or parsley.

If you plan to barbecue the steak, light the charcoal about 30 minutes before cooking time; to grill, pre-heat the grill for 10 minutes. With your fingers, rub the ginger and cayenne pepper into both sides of the steak, and allow it to stand at room temperature until you are ready to cook it.

Cook the steak on the first side for 6 minutes, then turn it, and sprinkle it with the salt. Grill the steak on the second side for 5 to 6 minutes for medium-rare meat. Transfer the steak to a platter and let it rest for about 5 minutes before carving it into thin slices. Serve the peach piccalilli on the side.

SUGGESTED ACCOMPANIMENTS: *sugar snap peas or mange-tout; wild rice.*

Beef Salad
with Carrots and Mint

Serves 6
Working time: about 40 minutes
Total time: about 3 hours (includes marinating)

Calories **255**
Protein **25g**
Cholesterol **65mg**
Total fat **11g**
Saturated fat **3g**
Sodium **340mg**

850 g	rump steak in one piece, trimmed of fat	1¾ lb
4 tbsp	unsalted brown stock or unsalted chicken stock (recipes, page 138)	4 tbsp
1½ tbsp	low-sodium soy sauce or shoyu	1½ tbsp
4 tbsp	fresh lime juice	4 tbsp
2	garlic cloves, finely chopped	2
2 tsp	sugar	2 tsp
	freshly ground black pepper	
2 tsp	chili paste, or ½ tsp hot red pepper flakes	2 tsp
2 tbsp	chopped fresh mint, or 2 tsp dried mint	2 tbsp
3	carrots	3
250 g	cucumber, thinly sliced	8 oz
1	sweet white onion, thinly sliced	1
6	cherry tomatoes, halved	6
250 g	daikon radish or ordinary radishes, shredded	8 oz
2 tbsp	safflower oil	2 tbsp

Set the steak in a baking dish. In a small bowl, combine the stock, soy sauce, 2 tablespoons of the lime juice, the garlic, sugar, some black pepper, the chili paste or red pepper flakes, and half of the mint. Pour this mixture over the steak and let it marinate at room temperature for 2 hours.

With a cannelle knife or a paring knife, cut several shallow lengthwise grooves in each carrot. Thinly slice the carrots and place the resulting flowers in a large bowl. Add the cucumber, onion, tomatoes and radish to the bowl with the carrots.

Remove the steak from the marinade and pat it dry with paper towels. Strain the marinade into a small saucepan and bring it to the boil. Remove the pan from the heat, whisk in the oil and the remaining 2 table-spoons of lime juice, and pour the dressing over the vegetables. Add the rest of the mint and toss well. Set the vegetables aside.

Grill the steak about 7.5 cm (3 inches) below a pre-heated grill until it is medium rare — 5 to 7 minutes per side. Transfer the steak to a cutting board and let it rest for 10 minutes, then slice it against the grain into thin pieces.

Using a slotted spoon, transfer the vegetables to a serving dish. Arrange the steak slices on top of the vegetables; pour the dressing left in the bowl over all, and serve at once.

SUGGESTED ACCOMPANIMENT: *poppy-seed rolls.*

Barbecued Steaks with Glazed Shallots and Mushrooms

Serves 4
Working time: about 20 minutes
Total time: about 40 minutes

Calories **290**
Protein **26g**
Cholesterol **60mg**
Total fat **9g**
Saturated fat **3g**
Sodium **210mg**

4	entrecôte or rump steaks (about 150 g/5 oz) each, trimmed of fat	4
2 tsp	safflower oil	2 tsp
250 g	mushrooms, wiped clean	8 oz
250 g	shallots, peeled	8 oz
2 tbsp	honey	2 tbsp
1 tsp	chopped fresh tarragon, or ½ tsp dried tarragon	1 tsp
12.5 cl	Madeira or port	4 fl oz
12.5 cl	unsalted brown or chicken stock (recipes, page 138)	4 fl oz
2 tsp	cornflour, mixed with 1 tbsp of the stock	2 tsp
¼ tsp	salt	¼ tsp
	freshly ground black pepper	

If you plan to barbecue the steaks, light the charcoal about 30 minutes before cooking time; to grill, pre-heat the grill for 10 minutes.

Heat the oil in a non-stick frying pan over medium heat; add the mushrooms and sauté them until they are lightly browned — about 4 minutes. Using a slotted spoon, transfer the mushrooms to a bowl. Pour ¼ litre (8 fl oz) of water into the pan and add the shallots, honey and tarragon. Partially cover the pan; bring the liquid to a simmer and cook the mixture until the shallots are translucent and only 4 tablespoons of liquid remains — 8 to 10 minutes.

Return the mushrooms to the pan and toss them with the shallots and the liquid until all are coated with a syrupy glaze — about 2 minutes longer. Keep the glazed shallots and mushrooms warm.

In a small saucepan, reduce the Madeira or port by half over medium-high heat. Add the stock and bring the mixture to a simmer. Whisk the cornflour mixture into the simmering liquid. Continue cooking the sauce until it thickens, and add ⅛ teaspoon of the salt and some pepper. Keep the sauce warm while you prepare the steaks.

Grill or barbecue the steaks for 3 minutes. Turn the steaks over and season them with the remaining ⅛ teaspoon of salt and some more pepper. Cook the steaks for 3 minutes longer for medium-rare meat. Serve the steaks with the glazed shallots and mushrooms on the side and the sauce poured on top.

SUGGESTED ACCOMPANIMENT: *steamed green beans.*

Low-Fat Hamburgers with Spicy Pumpkin Ketchup

THE RECIPE FOR PUMPKIN KETCHUP YIELDS MORE THAN
ENOUGH FOR EIGHT HAMBURGERS; THE EXCESS MAY BE STORED
IN THE REFRIGERATOR FOR UP TO ONE WEEK

Calories **275**
Protein **21g**
Cholesterol **45mg**
Total fat **5g**
Saturated fat **2g**
Sodium **155mg**

Serves 8
Working time: about 15 minutes
Total time: about 1 hour and 15 minutes

850 g	topside of beef, trimmed of fat and minced (box, left)	1¾ lb
225 g	burghul	7½ oz
2	garlic cloves, very finely chopped	2
25 g	fresh parsley, finely chopped	1 oz
2 tbsp	grainy mustard	2 tbsp
	Spicy pumpkin ketchup	
500 g	canned pumpkin	1 lb
1	onion, finely chopped	1
1	apple or pear, peeled, cored and chopped	1
12.5 cl	cider vinegar	4 fl oz
2 tbsp	sugar	2 tbsp
1 tbsp	honey	1 tbsp
½ tsp	ground cloves	½ tsp
½ tsp	curry powder	½ tsp
¼ tsp	ground allspice	¼ tsp
¼ tsp	cayenne pepper	¼ tsp
¼ tsp	salt	¼ tsp
	freshly ground black pepper	

Combine the ketchup ingredients in a non-reactive saucepan. Stir in ¼ litre (8 fl oz) of water and simmer the mixture over medium-low heat for 1 hour. Purée the ketchup in a food processor or a blender, then work it through a sieve with a wooden spoon. Transfer the ketchup to a serving bowl and set it aside.

While the ketchup is simmering, put the burghul into a heatproof bowl and pour 40 cl (13 fl oz) of boiling water over it. Cover the bowl and set it aside for 30 minutes. ▶

Guaranteeing Lean Mince Every Time

Beef and veal bought ready minced is often excessively fatty. Even what is labelled "lean" may not be as low in fat as you would like. There is a way, however, to guarantee a very lean product — buy a lean cut and ask the butcher to trim and **mince it for you. Or you can prepare it at home — either by hand, or using a mincing machine or a food processor. Because none of their precious juices have been pressed out, hamburgers are unusually delicious to eat when made with hand-minced beef.**

1 *SLICING THE MEAT. Trim off all the traces of fat and membrane from the meat — here a piece of corner topside — and cut the meat into uniform slices. Place the slices on top of one another and cut through to make evenly sized strips.*

2 *CUBING. Cut the strips of lean meat into fairly small cubes. The mincing will proceed more swiftly if you start with the meat in pieces of roughly equal size.*

3 *MINCING. Spread the cubed meat out evenly on a chopping board and chop it with a cleaver, or a matched pair of sharp, heavy knives. With a loose-wristed action, work the knives alternately and rhythmically, as if beating a drum (above, left). As the chopping progresses, the meat pieces will begin to spread out. Stop from time to time and use one of the knife blades to flip and turn the chopped mass back into the centre (above, right): this helps achieve a consistent texture. Continue chopping until the meat is minced as coarsely or finely as the recipe dictates.*

If you plan to barbecue the hamburgers, light the charcoal about 30 minutes before cooking time; to grill, preheat the grill for 10 minutes.

Put the minced beef, soaked burghul, garlic, parsley and mustard into a bowl, and combine them thoroughly by hand. Form the mixture into eight patties. Grill or barbecue the hamburgers for 3 to 4 minutes on each side for medium-rare meat. Serve the hamburgers hot with the ketchup alongside.

SUGGESTED ACCOMPANIMENTS: *poppy seed rolls; sliced tomatoes; lettuce leaves.*

Sirloin Barbecued in Garlic Smoke

Serves 6
Working time: about 30 minutes
Total time: about 45 minutes

Calories **220**
Protein **26g**
Cholesterol **75mg**
Total fat **11g**
Saturated fat **3g**
Sodium **105mg**

1 kg	sirloin steak in one piece, about 4 cm (1½ inches) thick, trimmed of fat	2 lb
10	unpeeled garlic cloves, crushed	10
	Onion-pepper relish	
2 tbsp	safflower oil	2 tbsp
1	small red onion, thinly sliced	1
1	garlic clove, finely chopped	1
1 tsp	finely chopped fresh ginger root	1 tsp
1	sweet green pepper, seeded, deribbed and julienned	1
2	spring onions, trimmed and thinly sliced	2
2 tbsp	rice vinegar or distilled white vinegar	2 tbsp
¼ tsp	sugar	¼ tsp
⅛ tsp	salt	⅛ tsp

About 30 minutes before cooking time, light the charcoal in the barbecue. Put the crushed garlic cloves in ¼ litre (8 fl oz) of cold water and let them soak while you make the relish.

Heat the oil in a heavy or non-stick frying pan over medium heat. Add the red onion slices and cook them, stirring frequently, until they have softened without losing their colour — 3 to 4 minutes. Add the chopped garlic and ginger, and cook the mixture for 30 seconds longer; transfer it to a bowl. Add the green pepper, spring onions, vinegar, sugar and salt; stir the relish and set it aside.

When the charcoal is hot, cook the steak for 7 minutes on the first side. Drain the water from the garlic cloves. Remove the steak from the barbecue and toss the soaked garlic cloves directly on to the charcoal; a garlicky smoke will curl up. Return the steak to the barbecue and cook it on the second side for 5 to 7 minutes longer for medium-rare meat.

Transfer the steak to a platter and let it rest for 5 minutes. Carve the steak into thin slices; spread the onion-pepper relish over each portion just before serving, or present the relish on the side.

SUGGESTED ACCOMPANIMENT: *baked jacket potatoes.*

Grilled Entrecôte Steaks with Fennel-Scented Vegetables

Serves 8
Working time: about 20 minutes
Total time: about 40 minutes

Calories **235**
Protein **26g**
Cholesterol **65mg**
Total fat **10g**
Saturated fat **39g**
Sodium **200mg**

4	thick entrecôte steaks (about 300 g/10 oz each), trimmed of fat	4
2 tbsp	olive oil	2 tbsp
1½ tsp	fennel seeds, lightly crushed	1½ tsp
3	garlic cloves, very thinly sliced	3
500 g	aubergine, cut into 1 cm (½ inch) cubes	1 lb
175 g	onion, chopped	6 oz
2 tbsp	fresh lemon juice	2 tbsp
750 g	ripe tomatoes, skinned, seeded and cut into 1 cm (½ inch) pieces	1½ lb
½ tsp	salt	½ tsp
	freshly ground black pepper	

If you plan to barbecue the steaks, light the charcoal about 30 minutes before cooking time; to grill, preheat the grill for about 10 minutes.

In the meantime, heat the olive oil in a large, heavy frying pan over high heat. When the oil is hot, add the fennel seeds and garlic, and cook them for 30 seconds, stirring constantly. Add the aubergine, onion and lemon juice and cook the vegetables for 5 minutes, stirring frequently. Next, add the tomatoes, ¼ teaspoon of the salt and a generous grinding of pepper to the pan. Cook the vegetable mixture for 3 to 4 minutes longer, stirring continuously. Cover the pan and set the mixture aside while you finish the dish.

Grill or barbecue the steaks for 3 to 4 minutes. Turn the steaks over and sprinkle them with the remaining ¼ teaspoon of salt and some pepper. Cook the steaks for an additional 3 to 4 minutes for medium-rare meat. Let the steaks stand for 5 minutes before thinly slicing them against the grain. Divide the meat and vegetables among eight dinner plates and serve at once.

SUGGESTED ACCOMPANIMENT: *steamed red potatoes.*

Grilled Roulades with Onion Compote

Serves 4
Working time: about 45 minutes
Total time: about 1 hour

Calories **230**
Protein **21g**
Cholesterol **45mg**
Total fat **5g**
Saturated fat **2g**
Sodium **305mg**

4	pieces of rump steak (about 125 g/4 oz each), trimmed of fat	4
600 g	pearl onions, blanched in boiling water for 5 minutes, drained and peeled	1¼ lb
75 g	sultanas	2½ oz
⅛ tsp	salt	⅛ tsp
1 tsp	red wine vinegar	1 tsp
4 tbsp	grainy mustard	4 tbsp
4 tbsp	finely chopped fresh parsley	4 tbsp
	freshly ground black pepper	

Put the onions, sultanas, salt, vinegar and ¼ litre (8 fl oz) of water into a heavy saucepan. Bring the liquid to the boil, then reduce the heat, and simmer the mixture until the onions are golden-brown and the liquid has evaporated — 15 to 20 minutes.

If you plan to barbecue the roulades, light the charcoal about 30 minutes before cooking time; to grill, preheat the grill for about 10 minutes.

While the onion compote is reducing, butterfly and pound the steaks as shown opposite. Mix the mustard, parsley and some pepper in a small bowl and spread this mixture over the meat. Roll each steak into a loose bundle; tie the roulades with butcher's string to hold them together.

When the onions finish cooking, set them aside and keep them warm.

Grill or barbecue the beef rolls for a total of 8 minutes, turning them every 2 minutes. Transfer the rolls to a platter; serve the onion compote alongside.

SUGGESTED ACCOMPANIMENT: *steamed Brussels sprouts.*

Butterflying and Pounding a Steak

1 *BUTTERFLYING A STEAK. Place a steak flat on a work surface. Using a thin-bladed knife, begin to halve the steak horizontally. Stop the knife just short of the far edge so that the upper and lower halves remain attached, like the wings of a butterfly.*

2 *POUNDING THE MEAT. Open out the butterflied steak and place it on a sheet of plastic film. Cover the steak with another piece of plastic film. Using a wooden bat or the flat of a large, heavy knife, pound the meat gently to the thickness called for in the recipe.*

Grilled Fillet Steaks with Roasted Garlic Sauce

Serves 4
Working time: about 30 minutes
Total time: about 50 minutes

Calories **170**
Protein **20g**
Cholesterol **55mg**
Total fat **6g**
Saturated fat **2g**
Sodium **100mg**

4	fillet steaks (125 g/4 oz each)	4
2	whole garlic bulbs, cloves separated but not peeled	2
½ tsp	juniper berries, crushed	½ tsp
1 tsp	cracked peppercorns	1 tsp
¼ litre	red wine	8 fl oz
3	shallots, sliced, or ½ small onion, finely chopped	3
½ litre	unsalted brown or chicken stock (recipes, page 138)	16 fl oz

Preheat the oven to 240°C (475°F or Mark 9).

Scatter the garlic cloves in a small baking dish and roast them until they are very soft — 20 to 30 minutes. Set the garlic cloves aside to cool.

If you plan to barbecue the steaks, light the charcoal about 30 minutes before cooking time; to grill, preheat the grill for about 10 minutes.

In a small bowl, mix together the juniper berries and pepper. Press the mixture into both sides of each of the steaks and set them aside at room temperature.

Pour the wine into a small, non-reactive saucepan and add the shallots or onion. Boil the mixture over medium-high heat until nearly all the liquid has evaporated — about 5 minutes. Add the stock, bring the liquid to the boil, and continue cooking it until it is reduced to about ¼ litre (8 fl oz) — about 5 minutes.

Squeeze the garlic pulp from the skins into a food processor or a blender. Pour in the stock and purée the garlic. Put the garlic sauce (it will be thick) into the saucepan and keep it warm.

Cook the steaks for approximately 3 minutes on each side for medium-rare meat. Serve the steaks with the garlic sauce.

SUGGESTED ACCOMPANIMENT: *oven-fried potatoes.*

South Seas Kebabs

Serves 4
Working time: about 35 minutes
Total time: about 2 hours and 30 minutes
(includes marinating)

Calories **180**
Protein **19g**
Cholesterol **45mg**
Total fat **4g**
Saturated fat **2g**
Sodium **195mg**

500 g	rump steak, trimmed of fat and cut into 2 cm (¾ inch) cubes	1 lb
1	ripe papaya, peeled, seeded and cut into 2.5 cm (1 inch) cubes	1
1	sweet red or green pepper, seeded, deribbed, cut into 2 cm (¾ inch) squares	1
Honey-ginger glaze		
17.5 cl	unsalted brown or chicken stock (recipes, page 138)	6 fl oz
1	spring onion, trimmed and thinly sliced	1
2	garlic cloves, finely chopped	2
2 tbsp	finely chopped fresh ginger root	2 tbsp
1 tbsp	honey	1 tbsp
¼ tsp	salt	¼ tsp
¼ tsp	cracked black peppercorns	¼ tsp
1 tbsp	cornflour mixed with 1 tbsp water	1 tbsp

Purée about one third of the papaya in a food processor

or a blender; set the remaining cubes aside. Mix the beef and the papaya purée in a shallow dish; cover the dish and marinate the beef in the refrigerator for about 2 hours.

If you plan to barbecue the kebabs, light the charcoal about 30 minutes before cooking time. To grill, preheat the grill for 10 minutes.

To prepare the glaze, combine the stock, spring onion, garlic, ginger, honey, salt and cracked peppercorns in a small saucepan over medium heat. Bring the mixture to a simmer and cook it for 3 to 4 minutes. Stir in the cornflour mixture and continue cooking and stirring the glaze until it thickens — 1 to 2 minutes. Remove the glaze from the heat and set it aside.

To assemble the kebabs, thread the cubes of beef, papaya and pepper on to four 30 cm (12 inch) skewers. Cook the kebabs for 3 minutes. Turn them and cook them for 3 minutes more. Brush some glaze over the kebabs and cook them for 1 minute. Turn the kebabs once more, brush them with the glaze, and cook them for another minute. Transfer the kebabs to a serving platter and brush them with the remaining glaze; serve the kebabs immediately.

SUGGESTED ACCOMPANIMENT: *saffron rice tossed with peas.*

Marinated Beef Salad with Potatoes and French Beans

Serves 4
Working time: about 25 minutes
Total time: about 3 hours (includes marinating)

Calories **295**			
Protein **29g**	600 g	sirloin steak, about 2.5 cm (1 inch) thick, trimmed of fat	1 ¼ lb
Cholesterol **75mg**	1	small onion, thinly sliced	1
Total fat **11g**	1	garlic clove, finely chopped	1
Saturated fat **3g**	½	sweet green pepper, finely chopped	½
Sodium **150mg**	⅛ tsp	cracked black peppercorns	⅛ tsp
	1 tbsp	chopped fresh tarragon, or 1 tsp dried tarragon	1 tbsp
	2	lemons, juice only	2
	250 g	waxy potatoes, scrubbed and cut into 2.5 cm (1 inch) cubes	8 oz
	350 g	French beans, trimmed	12 oz
	⅛ tsp	salt	⅛ tsp
	1	ripe tomato, cut into wedges	1
	4 tsp	safflower oil	4 tsp
	1 tsp	Dijon mustard	1 tsp

In a small bowl, combine the onion, garlic, green pepper, black peppercorns and tarragon. Scatter half of the mixture on the bottom of a shallow non-reactive pan. Put the steak into the pan and sprinkle the rest of the mixture on top. Pour the lemon juice over the steak and let it marinate for 2 hours at room temperature or overnight in the refrigerator.

Cook the potatoes in a saucepan of boiling water until they are tender — 7 to 10 minutes. Drain them and set them aside to cool. Pour enough water into the saucepan to fill it to a depth of 2.5 cm (1 inch). Set a steamer in the pan and bring the water to the boil over medium-high heat. Add the beans to the steamer, cover the pan, and steam the beans until they are just tender — about 5 minutes. Refresh the beans under cold running water, drain them well, and put them into a large salad bowl.

Preheat the grill. Remove the steak from the marinade and pour the marinade into a small saucepan. Scrape any clinging marinade ingredients off the steak into the saucepan. Bring the liquid to the boil and cook it for 2 minutes. Set it aside.

Pat the steak dry with paper towels and grill it for 4 minutes on the first side. Sprinkle the steak with the salt, turn the steak over and grill it for about 4 minutes longer for medium-rare meat.

Let the steak rest at room temperature for 30 minutes, then slice it into thin strips. Cut each strip into 5 cm (2 inch) lengths. Add the beef, the cooled potatoes and the tomatoes to the beans.

Strain the marinade into a small bowl, discarding the solids left in the sieve. Whisk the oil and the mustard into the bowl to make a vinaigrette. Pour the vinaigrette over the salad and toss well. Refrigerate the salad for 20 minutes before serving it.

Grilled Beef and Fresh Salsa in Flour Tortillas

Serves 4
Working (and total) time: about 1 hour

Calories **375**
Protein **27g**
Cholesterol **60mg**
Total fat **10g**
Saturated fat **2g**
Sodium **185mg**

500g	rump steak, trimmed of fat	1 lb
2 tbsp	fresh lime juice	2 tbsp
2 tbsp	tequila or gin	2 tbsp
½ tsp	chili powder	½ tsp
½ tsp	dried oregano	½ tsp
¼ tsp	ground cumin	¼ tsp
	freshly ground black pepper	
8	spring onions, green tops trimmed to 7.5 cm (3 inches) in length	8
8	flour tortillas, 25 cm (10 inches) in diameter	8
110 g	cos lettuce, shredded	4 oz

Salsa		
500 g	ripe tomatoes, preferably plum tomatoes, skinned, seeded and finely chopped	1 lb
1	sweet green pepper, seeded, deribbed and finely diced	1
1	small onion, finely chopped	1
1 to 3	fresh green chili peppers, seeded and finely chopped (caution, page 8)	1 to 3
2 tbsp	fresh lime juice	2 tbsp
2 tbsp	chopped fresh coriander	2 tbsp
¼ tsp	salt	¼ tsp

Slice the steak against the grain into 1 cm (½ inch) wide strips. In a large, shallow dish, combine the lime juice, tequila or gin, chili powder, oregano, cumin and black pepper. Add the steak strips and the spring onions, and toss them well. Let the steak marinate at room temperature for 20 minutes.

Combine the salsa ingredients in a bowl; let the salsa

stand for at least 15 minutes to blend the flavours.

If you plan to barbecue the meat, light the charcoal about 30 minutes before cooking time; to grill, preheat the grill for about 10 minutes.

Stack the tortillas and wrap them in aluminium foil. Warm the tortillas in a preheated 180°C (350°F or Mark 4) oven for 10 minutes. Meanwhile, cook the steak strips in the centre of the grill or barbecue with the spring onions laid carefully at the side, for 1 minute per side; the steak should be medium rare and the spring onions lightly charred. Cut the steak strips into pieces about 2.5 cm (1 inch) long.

To serve, place equal amounts of steak pieces and their juices on the tortillas. Add some lettuce and a spring onion to each tortilla, then spoon some of the salsa over the top. Roll up the tortillas and serve them at once; serve any remaining salsa separately.

SUGGESTED ACCOMPANIMENT: *black beans and rice.*

EDITOR'S NOTE: *To make flour tortillas, if ready-made ones are not available, rub 90 g (3 oz) of white vegetable fat into 400 g (14 oz) of plain flour mixed with 1 teaspoon of salt. Gradually add about 17.5 cl (6 fl oz) of warm water and knead into a dough — about 1 minute. Add more flour if the dough is sticky, or more water if it is too dry. Rest the dough for 15 to 20 minutes. Divide it into eight, and roll each piece out on a floured worktop to make a 25 cm (10 inch) circle, 4 mm (⅛ inch) thick. Fry each tortilla in a lightly greased crêpe or frying pan until bubbles form and the surface is lightly speckled — about 30 seconds. Using a wooden spoon or spatula, flatten the bubbles, then turn the tortilla over and cook for 30 seconds on the other side.*

Sirloin and Leek Kebabs

Serves 4
Working (and total) time: about 1 hour

Calories **335**
Protein **28g**
Cholesterol **75mg**
Total fat **7g**
Saturated fat **3g**
Sodium **210mg**

600 g	sirloin steak, trimmed of fat and cut into long, thin, 1 cm (½ inch) wide strips	1¼ lb
½ tsp	ground white pepper	½ tsp
1 tsp	cayenne pepper	1 tsp
½ tsp	ground allspice	½ tsp
½ tsp	ground cumin	½ tsp
½ tsp	turmeric	½ tsp
¼ tsp	salt	¼ tsp
3	leeks, washed thoroughly to remove all grit, white parts cut into 1 cm (½ inch) wide strips, green parts reserved for another use	3
Ginger chutney		
75 g	sultanas	2½ oz
5 cm	fresh ginger root, peeled and chopped	2 inch
½	small onion, chopped	½
1	tart apple, cored and quartered	1
12.5 cl	fresh lime juice	4 fl oz
1 tbsp	honey	1 tbsp
¼ tsp	whole mustard seeds	¼ tsp

To make the chutney, chop the sultanas, ginger, onion, apple, lime juice, honey and mustard seeds in a food processor or a blender. Transfer the chutney to a bowl and refrigerate it.

If you plan to barbecue the kebabs, light the charcoal about 30 minutes before cooking time; to grill, preheat the grill for about 10 minutes.

Combine the white pepper, cayenne pepper, allspice, cumin, turmeric and salt in a small bowl. Spread the strips of beef on a baking sheet or tray. With your fingers, rub the spice mixture into the beef. Set the beef aside.

Blanch the leeks in a large saucepan of boiling water for 2 minutes. Drain them and refresh them under cold running water, then drain them again.

Lay a strip of leek on top of each piece of meat. Divide the meat and leeks among 12 skewers, threading the skewer through both leek and meat at frequent intervals.

Barbecue or grill the kebabs for 1 minute on each side for medium-rare meat, and serve them with the ginger chutney.

SUGGESTED ACCOMPANIMENT: *steamed rice tossed with peas*

Barbecued Beef Stuffed with Summer Vegetables

Serves 8
Working time: about 1 hour
Total time: about 2 hours (includes marinating)

Calories **210**
Protein **27g**
Cholesterol **75mg**
Total fat **9g**
Saturated fat **3g**
Sodium **190mg**

1.25 kg	rump steak in one piece, about 5 cm (2 inches) thick, trimmed of fat	2½ lb
1 tsp	Dijon mustard	1 tsp
¼ tsp	freshly ground black pepper	¼ tsp
1	garlic clove, crushed	1
⅛ tsp	salt	⅛ tsp
4 tbsp	red wine	4 tbsp
Vegetable stuffing		
1 tbsp	olive oil	1 tbsp
60 g	onion, chopped	2 oz
1	sweet green pepper, seeded, deribbed and diced	1
1	sweet red pepper, seeded, deribbed and diced	1
60 g	courgettes, preferably mixed green and yellow, diced	2 oz
2	garlic cloves, finely chopped	2
1½ tsp	fresh thyme, or ½ tsp dried thyme	1½ tsp
1½ tsp	chopped fresh oregano, or ½ tsp dried oregano	1½ tsp
¼ tsp	hot red pepper flakes	¼ tsp
¼ tsp	salt	¼ tsp
	freshly ground black pepper	
30 g	fresh breadcrumbs	1 oz

Using the technique shown on the right, cut a pocket in the beef. Combine the mustard, pepper, garlic, salt and wine in a shallow dish. Add the steak to the dish and turn the meat in the marinade once to coat it evenly. Marinate the steak for 1 hour at room temperature or about 3 hours in the refrigerator, turning it several times.

Meanwhile, make the stuffing. Heat the oil in a large heavy frying pan over low heat. Add the onion, green and red peppers, courgettes and garlic. Partially cover the pan and cook the vegetables, stirring frequently, until they begin to soften — about 7 minutes. Add the thyme, oregano, red pepper flakes, salt and some black pepper. Stir the mixture well and remove it from the heat. Add the breadcrumbs and toss them with the vegetables. Allow the mixture to cool.

About 30 minutes before cooking the meat, light the charcoal. When the charcoal is nearly ready, remove the meat from the dish, reserving the marinade. Stuff the beef with the cooled vegetable mixture and tie it as demonstrated below.

When the charcoal is hot, bank it against the sides of the barbecue. Place a foil drip pan in the centre of the grate and set the rack in place. Lay the meat in the centre of the rack. Cook the meat, basting it occasionally with the reserved marinade, for 20 minutes. Turn the meat over and continue cooking it for 10 to 20 minutes longer for medium-rare meat.

Remove the meat from the barbecue and let it stand for 30 minutes. Discard the strings and slice the meat across the grain. Arrange the slices on a platter and serve immediately. This dish can also be prepared ahead of time and served cold.

SUGGESTED ACCOMPANIMENTS: *barbecued sliced potatoes; spinach salad.*

Cutting and Stuffing a Pocket in a Rump Steak

1 *CUTTING A POCKET. Insert the tip of a knife (here, a boning knife) into the side of a 5 cm (2 inch) thick boneless rump steak. Cut in as deeply as possible without piercing the outer edge of the meat to form a pocket.*

2 *STUFFING THE POCKET. Use your fingers to stuff the prepared filling (recipe, left) into the pocket. Be sure to push the filling in deep.*

3 *MAKING THE FIRST LOOP. To keep the pocket from opening during cooking, tie the piece as you would a roast. First, loop string round one end of the steak and knot it, leaving a length of string loose at that end.*

4 *MAKING SUCCESSIVE LOOPS. With the string still attached to the ball, form a loose loop and twist it round twice. Bring the loop over and under the other end of the meat.*

5 *TIGHTENING THE STRING. Slide the loop forwards so that it rests about 4 to 5 cm (1½ to 2 inches) in front of the first loop, and tighten it by pulling both ends of the string at once. Repeat the process, making three or more loops round the meat and tightening the string after each loop.*

6 *TYING THE JOINT TOGETHER. Finally, draw the string under the entire length of the meat and back to the first loop you made. Knot the string to the loose length at that end, then sever the string from the ball.*

Tournedos with Pepper Sauces

Serves 4
Working time: about 1 hour
Total time: about 2 hours and 15 minutes
(includes marinating)

Calories **280**
Protein **26g**
Cholesterol **75mg**
Total fat **12g**
Saturated fat **4g**
Sodium **190mg**

600 g	beef fillet, trimmed of fat and cut into eight small steaks	1¼ lb
1	garlic clove, finely chopped	1
¼ litre	red wine	8 fl oz
30 g	fresh rosemary sprigs, or 1½ tbsp dried rosemary	1 oz
3	sweet yellow or green peppers	3
3	sweet red peppers	3
2 tsp	red wine vinegar	2 tsp
¼ tsp	salt	¼ tsp
1	large aubergine (about 500 g/1 lb), sliced into eight rounds	1
1 tbsp	olive oil	1 tbsp
8	fresh rosemary sprigs for garnish (optional)	8

Put the steaks into a shallow dish large enough to hold them in a single layer. Sprinkle the garlic, wine and rosemary over the steaks and set them aside to marinate at room temperature for 2 hours.

About 1 hour before the steaks finish marinating, cook the peppers under a preheated grill, turning them frequently until their skins blister — about 8 minutes. Transfer the peppers to a large bowl and cover the bowl with plastic film — the trapped steam will loosen the skins. When the peppers are cool enough to handle, peel, seed and derib them over a sieve set in a bowl to catch the juices. Cut one of the yellow or green peppers and one of the red peppers into 5 mm (¼ inch) dice; reserve the dice for garnish.

Purée the remaining two yellow or green peppers in a blender or a food processor. Add to the purée 1 teaspoon of the vinegar, ⅛ teaspoon of the salt and half of the accumulated pepper juices. Pour the purée into a small saucepan and set it aside.

Purée the remaining two red peppers in the blender or food processor; add the remaining vinegar, salt and pepper juices, and pour this purée into a second small saucepan. Warm both sauces over medium-low heat while you prepare the aubergine and steaks.

With a paring knife, score both sides of each aubergine slice in a crosshatch pattern. Lightly brush both sides with the oil, then grill the slices until they are soft and browned — 2 to 3 minutes per side. Remove the slices from the grill and keep them warm.

Take the steaks out of the marinade and pat them dry; discard the marinade. Grill the steaks until they are medium rare — about 3 minutes per side.

Place two aubergine slices on each of four dinner plates. Set a steak on each aubergine slice and spoon the warmed pepper sauces round the steaks. Garnish each portion with the reserved diced peppers — and, if you are using it, a sprig of fresh rosemary — just before serving.

SUGGESTED ACCOMPANIMENT: *rye bread.*

Fillet Steaks Stuffed with Oysters and Topped with Kale

THIS DISH IS A VARIATION OF THE AUSTRALIAN SPECIALITY, CARPET BAG STEAK.

Serves 6
Working (and total) time: about 1 hour

Calories **185**
Protein **23g**
Cholesterol **75mg**
Total fat **6g**
Saturated fat **2g**
Sodium **195mg**

6	fillet steaks (about 125 g/4 oz each), trimmed of fat	6
12	shucked oysters, with their liquid	12
6	shallots, finely chopped	6
3 tbsp	white wine vinegar or red wine vinegar	3 tbsp
4 tbsp	unsalted brown or chicken stock (recipes, page 138)	4 tbsp
250 g	kale, coarsely shredded	8 oz
¼ tsp	salt	¼ tsp
	freshly ground black pepper	

If you plan to barbecue the steaks, light the charcoal about 30 minutes before cooking time; to grill, preheat the grill for about 10 minutes.

Poach the oysters in their liquid in a small saucepan over medium heat just until their edges curl — about 1 minute. With a slotted spoon, remove the oysters from the pan and set them aside. Strain the poaching ▶

liquid and reserve it.

Cut a slit in the side of each steak to make a pocket large enough to hold one of the oysters. Stuff the steaks with six of the oysters.

Cook the steaks on the barbecue or under the grill for 2 to 3 minutes on each side for medium-rare steaks. Set the steaks aside in a warm place.

Heat the shallots, vinegar and stock in a large heavy frying pan over medium-high heat until the liquid boils. Continue cooking the mixture until it has reduced by one third — 3 to 4 minutes. Stir in the kale, the remaining oysters, the poaching liquid, the salt and some pepper. Toss the mixture until the greens begin to wilt — about 2 minutes.

Spoon the kale and oysters over the steaks and serve immediately.

SUGGESTED ACCOMPANIMENT: *baked potatoes*.

Skewered Beef with Julienned Papaya

Serves 8 as a main course or 16 as a starter
Working time: about 35 minutes
Total time: about 1 hour and 35 minutes
(includes marinating)

Calories **265**
Protein **25g**
Cholesterol **55mg**
Total fat **10g**
Saturated fat **3g**
Sodium **280mg**

1 kg	rump steak, trimmed of fat	2 lb
2	underripe papayas, or 4 mangoes, peeled, halved, seeded and julienned	2
2 tbsp	fresh lime juice	2 tbsp
32	cherry tomatoes, halved lengthwise	32
2	spring onions, green parts only, thinly sliced	2
2 tbsp	crushed unsalted roasted peanuts	2 tbsp
Spicy peanut marinade		
2½ tbsp	low-sodium soy sauce or shoyu	2½ tbsp
2	spring onions, white parts only, thinly sliced	2
1½ tbsp	finely chopped fresh ginger root	1½ tbsp
3	garlic cloves, finely chopped	3
2	small dried red chili peppers, chopped (caution, page 8), or ¼ tsp dried hot red pepper flakes	2
3 tbsp	peanut butter	3 tbsp
4 tbsp	plain low-fat yogurt	4 tbsp
2 tbsp	dry white wine	2 tbsp
2 tbsp	fresh lime juice	2 tbsp
1 tbsp	honey	1 tbsp

To make the marinade, combine the soy sauce with the spring onions, ginger, garlic, and chili peppers or pepper flakes in a large bowl. Let the mixture stand for 1 minute, then whisk in the peanut butter, yogurt, wine, lime juice and honey.

Slice the beef into strips about 12.5 cm (5 inches) long and 3 mm (⅛ inch) thick — you will need at least 32 slices. Toss the meat in the marinade and allow it to sit for 1 hour at room temperature.

While the beef is marinating, combine the papaya or mango julienne and the lime juice in a bowl. Refrigerate the fruit mixture.

If you plan to barbecue the beef, prepare the coals about 30 minutes before cooking time; to grill, preheat the grill for 10 minutes.

Insert a wooden skewer through a tomato half, then thread it through a strip of beef; finish with another tomato half. Repeat the process for the remaining tomatoes and beef. Brush the skewered meat and tomatoes with any remaining marinade.

Cook the meat in two batches until it begins to brown — 4 to 6 minutes. (Because the slices are so thin, the beef need be cooked on one side only.) Transfer the skewers to a serving platter.

Sprinkle the meat with the sliced spring onion greens and crushed peanuts, and serve the chilled papaya or mango alongside.

SUGGESTED ACCOMPANIMENT: *roasted sweet peppers*.

Veal Steaks Teriyaki

THIS RECIPE IS BASED ON THE JAPANESE "TERIYAKI" STYLE OF
MARINATING MEAT IN A MIXTURE OF MIRIN, SOY SAUCE AND
FRESH GINGER. THE LONG MARINATING TENDERIZES THE MEAT,
WITH SUCCULENT RESULTS.

Serves 6
Working time: about 10 minutes
Total time: about 25 hours (includes marinating)

Calories **185**
Protein **26g**
Cholesterol **90mg**
Total fat **7g**
Saturated fat **2g**
Sodium **150mg**

500 g	veal fillet in one piece, cut diagonally into eight pieces	1 lb
6 cl	low-sodium soy sauce or shoyu	2 fl oz
2 tbsp	mirin (Japanese sweet rice wine) or sweet sherry	2 tbsp
30 g	fresh ginger root, peeled and finely chopped	1 oz
4	garlic cloves, crushed	4
1 tsp	soft brown sugar	1 tsp
1 tbsp	groundnut oil	1 tbsp
15 cl	unsalted chicken stock (recipe, page 138)	¼ pint
	spring onions or celery cut into brushes for garnish	

In a jug, whisk the soy sauce with the mirin or sherry, ginger, garlic and sugar. Put the pieces of veal in a shallow dish and pour over the marinade. Turn the veal several times to ensure that the pieces are evenly coated. Cover and leave to marinate in the refrigerator for 24 to 36 hours, turning the meat occasionally. Thirty minutes before cooking, remove the veal from the refrigerator and let it come to room temperature. Ten minutes before cooking, preheat the grill.

Remove the veal from the marinade, brushing off and reserving any excess marinade. Brush the veal on both sides with the oil, then place the veal on the grill rack. Grill for 3 to 4 minutes, turn and grill for another 3 to 4 minutes.

Meanwhile, transfer the marinade to a small saucepan and add the stock. Bring the liquid to the boil, skim it, then simmer gently. Serve the veal steaks hot with the sauce poured over, garnished with spring onion or celery brushes.

SUGGESTED ACCOMPANIMENTS: *rice; stir-fried mange-tout with sweet red peppers.*

Veal Chops Dijonnaise

Serves 4
Working time: about 15 minutes
Total time: about 2 hours and 30 minutes
(includes marinating)

Calories **255**			
Protein **23g**	4	veal chops, each weighing 175 to 200 g (6 to 7 oz), trimmed of fat	4
Cholesterol **120mg**			
Total fat **16g**	3 tbsp	capers, drained and crushed	3 tbsp
Saturated fat **5g**	2 tbsp	virgin olive oil	2 tbsp
Sodium **120mg**	2 tbsp	fresh lemon juice	2 tbsp
	2 tsp	Dijon mustard	2 tsp
	2 tsp	chopped fresh tarragon, or 1 tsp dried tarragon	2 tsp
		freshly ground black pepper	
		fresh tarragon sprigs (optional)	

Place the chops side by side in a shallow dish. Put the capers, oil, lemon juice, mustard, chopped tarragon and some pepper in a jug and whisk them together. Brush the mixture over both sides of the chops. Cover and leave to marinate in a cold place for 2 hours.

Preheat the grill. Place the chops on the grill rack and grill for 10 minutes, basting frequently with the marinade. Turn the chops over and grill for another 10 minutes, again basting them with the marinade. Pour over the cooking juices from the grill pan and garnish with the tarragon sprigs, if using. Serve hot.

SUGGESTED ACCOMPANIMENTS: *seasonal green salad; mushrooms cooked in lemon juice.*

Paupiettes of Veal in Avgolemono Sauce

THE SAUCE IS BASED ON THE GREEK EGG AND LEMON SOUP OF THE SAME NAME: ITS RATHER SHARP, LEMONY FLAVOUR ADDS PIQUANCY TO THE VEAL AND STUFFING.

Serves 4
Working (and total) time: about 1 hour

Calories **285**			
Protein **28g**	4	veal escalopes, each weighing 90 to 125 g (3 to 4 oz), trimmed of fat, flattened (Step 1, overleaf)	4
Cholesterol **135mg**			
Total fat **11g**	3	small red onions, quartered	3
Saturated fat **3g**	1 tbsp	virgin olive oil	1 tbsp
Sodium **355mg**		freshly ground black pepper	
	Anchovy stuffing		
	6	canned anchovy fillets, soaked in 6 tbsp of milk for 20 minutes, drained, rinsed and patted dry	6
	150 g	fresh granary breadcrumbs	5 oz
	1	lemon, grated rind only	1
	2 tbsp	lemon juice	2 tbsp
	4 tsp	chopped fresh chervil or parsley (or mixture of the two)	4 tsp
		freshly ground black pepper	
	Avgolemono sauce		
	30 cl	unsalted chicken stock (recipe, page 138)	½ pint
	1	egg yolk	1
	1	lemon, juice only	1
	1 tsp	arrowroot	1 tsp
		freshly ground black pepper	

Cut each escalope into four equal-sized pieces *(Step 2, overleaf)*, making 16 pieces in all.

To make the stuffing, coarsely chop the anchovy fillets and put them in a bowl. Add the breadcrumbs, lemon rind and juice, chervil or parsley and some pepper. Preheat the grill. Spoon one sixteenth of the stuffing on to each piece of veal.

Roll the veal up round the stuffing, tucking in any ends of meat if necessary *(Step 3, overleaf)*, then squeeze the paupiettes gently in your hands so that they hold together. Thread four paupiettes on to each of four metal skewers, alternating with onion quarters. Place the skewers on the grill rack, brush with half the oil and sprinkle with some pepper. Grill for 2 to 3 minutes. Turn, brush with the remaining oil, sprinkle with pepper and grill for a further 2 to 3 minutes.

To make the sauce, put the stock in a small saucepan and bring to the boil. Remove from the heat. In a bowl, mix together the egg yolk, lemon juice and arrowroot. Stir in a few spoonfuls of the hot stock, then pour this mixture into the remaining stock in the pan. Bring to just below boiling point and simmer, whisking vigorously, until the sauce thickens — 2 to 3 minutes. Add some pepper to taste.

Pour some sauce on to individual plates and arrange the paupiettes and onions on top.

SUGGESTED ACCOMPANIMENTS: *watercress and green grape salad; tomato salad.*

Flattening, Stuffing and Rolling Veal Slices

1 *FLATTENING THE MEAT. Trim each escalope of excess fat and lay it between two sheets of plastic film. With a meat bat, flatten the escalope by gently tapping until the meat is of an even thickness. Vigorous pounding is unnecessary and will render the veal dry.*

2 *SLICING THE ESCALOPES. Cut each flattened escalope into four pieces. Put about a tablespoon of stuffing on one end of a piece.*

3 *ROLLING AND CURING. Roll up the meat, starting at the end nearest the stuffing. Squeeze the roll gently to help the stuffing adhere to the meat. Secure the rolls with a kebab skewer (recipe, page 31), or alternatively, pin each one with a toothpick.*

Barbecued Veal with Spicy Orange Sauce

Serves 8
Working time: about 1 hour
Total time: about 3 hours (includes marinating)

Calories **230**
Protein **22g**
Cholesterol **90mg**
Total fat **10g**
Saturated fat **3g**
Sodium **160mg**

1 kg	veal rump in one piece, trimmed	2 lb
1 tsp	allspice	1 tsp
1 tsp	juniper berries	1 tsp
2 tbsp	virgin olive oil	2 tbsp
¼ tsp	salt	¼ tsp
	freshly ground black pepper	
2	oranges, finely grated rind only	2
	Spicy orange sauce	
¼ litre	fresh orange juice	8 fl oz
4 tbsp	clear honey	4 tbsp
2 tbsp	red wine vinegar	2 tbsp
2	garlic cloves, crushed	2
400 g	canned tomatoes, drained and sieved	14 oz
1 tbsp	Grand Marnier	1 tbsp
½ tsp	paprika	½ tsp
	Tabasco sauce	
¼ tsp	salt	¼ tsp
	freshly ground black pepper	

To prepare the marinade, crush the allspice and juniper berries together with a pestle and mortar, then blend in the oil, salt, some pepper and the grated orange rind.

Place the veal joint in a shallow dish, pour the marinade over it and coat well. Cover and marinate at room temperature for 2 to 3 hours.

To prepare the sauce, put the orange juice, honey, wine vinegar, garlic, tomatoes and Grand Marnier in a heavy-bottomed saucepan. Add the paprika, a few drops of Tabasco sauce, the salt and some pepper. Bring to the boil, then lower the heat and simmer very gently for 45 minutes to 1 hour, until the sauce is reduced and thickened.

Light the charcoal in the barbecue about 30 minutes before cooking time. Skewer the veal into a neat shape using one or two large skewers. Cook on a rack over hot, but not fierce, coals, turning frequently until cooked through but still slightly pink inside — 35 to 45 minutes — taking care that the veal does not burn.

To serve, carefully slide the veal off the skewers on to a cutting board then cut into thin slices. Serve with the spicy orange sauce.

SUGGESTED ACCOMPANIMENTS: *green salad; granary bread.*
EDITOR'S NOTE: *The sauce can be served either hot or cold.*

Grilled Cutlets with Shallots and Fennel

Serves 4
Working (and total) time: about 35 minutes

Calories **265**
Protein **25g**
Cholesterol **110mg**
Total fat **15g**
Saturated fat **5g**
Sodium **260mg**

4	veal cutlets (about 250 g/8 oz each), cut between the bones, about 1 cm (½ inch) thick	4
2 tbsp	virgin olive oil	2 tbsp
1 tsp	grated lemon rind	1 tsp
½	lemon, juice only	½
1	large garlic clove, finely chopped	1
45 g	shallots, finely chopped	1½ oz
1 tbsp	chopped parsley	1 tbsp
1 tsp	chopped fresh rosemary, or ½ tsp dried rosemary, crumbled	1 tsp
	freshly ground black pepper	
90 g	bulb fennel, very finely julienned	3 oz
350 g	spring greens, washed, trimmed and finely shredded	12 oz
¼ tsp	salt	¼ tsp
	lemon wedges for garnish	

Preheat the grill. Combine the oil, lemon rind and juice, garlic, shallots, parsley, rosemary and some pepper in a small bowl. Arrange the cutlets side by side on a rack in a grill pan. Brush the tops with about a quarter of the lemon-shallot mixture and grill for about 8 minutes or until golden-brown. Turn the cutlets over and brush with another quarter of the lemon-shallot mixture. Grill for a further 5 minutes.

Mix the fennel into the remaining lemon-shallot mixture and pile on top of the cutlets. Press down lightly to smooth out any pieces of fennel that might be sticking up. Continue grilling for about 5 minutes or until the fennel mixture is golden-brown.

Meanwhile, cook the shredded spring greens in a vegetable steamer for 2 to 3 minutes, or until just tender. Add the salt to the greens and toss.

Spread out the greens in an even layer on a large serving platter. Arrange the cutlets on top and garnish with lemon wedges. Serve hot.

SUGGESTED ACCOMPANIMENT: *boiled new potatoes.*

Veal and Aubergine Kebabs with Strawberry and Cucumber Sauce

Serves 4
Working time: about 1 hour
Total time: about 1 hour and 40 minutes

Calories **200**
Protein **25g**
Cholesterol **75mg**
Total fat **5g**
Saturated fat **2g**
Sodium **295mg**

175 g	veal topside or top rump, trimmed of fat and minced (page 15)	6 oz
1	small aubergine (about 175 g/6 oz), peeled and chopped	1
1¼ tsp	salt	1¼ tsp
1	large sweet red pepper	1
1	garlic clove, chopped	1
175 g	chicken breast meat, minced	6 oz
	freshly ground black pepper	
½	lemon, grated rind only	½
2 tbsp	chopped fresh mint	2 tbsp
1 tbsp	chopped parsley	1 tbsp
60 to 90 g	fresh breadcrumbs	2 to 3 oz
8	large black olives, stoned	8
Strawberry and cucumber sauce		
125 g	cucumber	4 oz
15 cl	plain low-fat yogurt	¼ pint
45 g	strawberries, hulled and finely chopped	1½ oz
2 tbsp	finely sliced fresh mint	2 tbsp

Put the aubergine in a colander, sprinkle over 1 teaspoon of the salt and weight down with a plate. Leave to drain for 20 minutes.

Meanwhile, make the sauce. Grate the cucumber, then wrap it in paper towels and squeeze out excess moisture. Put the cucumber into a bowl, add the yogurt, strawberries and mint, and stir together. Cover and chill.

Place the pepper about 5 cm (2 inches) below a preheated grill, turning it from time to time until the skin becomes blistered. Put the pepper in a bowl, cover with plastic film and leave to cool; the steam trapped inside will loosen the skin. Peel the pepper, remove the stem, ribs and seeds, and cut it into 2.5 cm (1 inch) squares.

To make the kebabs, rinse the aubergine and squeeze it dry in your hands. Put the aubergine in a food processor, add the garlic and blend until smooth. Transfer the aubergine purée to a bowl and add the veal, chicken, remaining salt, some black pepper, the lemon rind, mint and parsley. Mix well together with your hands, then work in enough breadcrumbs to firm the mixture. Shape into walnut-size balls and chill for 30 minutes.

Preheat the grill. Thread the meatballs, squares of red pepper and the olives on to four or eight skewers. Grill for 15 to 20 minutes, turning the skewers to cook and brown evenly.

Serve the kebabs immediately accompanied by the strawberry and cucumber sauce.

SUGGESTED ACCOMPANIMENTS: *green salad; pitta bread.*

EDITOR'S NOTE: *These kebabs can also be cooked over a barbecue.*

Veal and Apricot Brochettes Tikka-Style

Serves 4
Working time: about 30 minutes
Total time: about 6 hours and 45 minutes
(includes marinating)

Calories **180**
Protein **20g**
Cholesterol **75mg**
Total fat **5g**
Saturated fat **2g**
Sodium **240mg**

350 g	veal topside, top rump or boned loin, trimmed of fat and cut into 2.5 cm (1 inch) cubes	12 oz
60 g	ready-to-eat dried apricots (about 8), halved	2 oz
250 g	courgettes, trimmed and cut into chunks	8 oz
	lime wedges or slices for garnish	
	Spicy yogurt marinade	
30 cl	plain low-fat yogurt	½ pint
1	small onion, chopped	1
1	garlic clove, chopped	1
1 cm	fresh ginger root, peeled, or 1 tbsp freshly grated ginger root	½ inch
1	lime, juice only	1
2	cardamom pods	2
1	small dried red chili pepper (caution, page 8)	1
4	cloves	4
6	black peppercorns	6
5 mm	piece cinnamon stick	¼ inch
1	piece of nutmeg, about the size of a hazelnut, or 1 tsp freshly grated nutmeg	1
¼ tsp	coriander seeds	¼ tsp
¼ tsp	cumin seeds	¼ tsp
¼ tsp	salt	¼ tsp

Combine the yogurt, onion, garlic, ginger and lime juice in a food processor and blend until quite smooth. Strain into a bowl.

Break open the cardamom pods and put the seeds in a mortar. Add the chili pepper, cloves, peppercorns, cinnamon stick, nutmeg, coriander seeds and cumin seeds. Pound with a pestle until fine. Alternatively, the spices may be worked in a spice grinder. Add the spices and the salt to the yogurt mixture and stir well. Add the cubes of veal and the apricots, and coat them in the mixture. Cover and leave to marinate in the refrigerator for at least 6 hours, stirring occasionally.

Preheat the grill. Thread the veal cubes, apricots and courgettes on to four or eight skewers, shaking off and reserving excess marinade. Grill the kebabs for about 15 minutes, turning them to cook and brown evenly.

While the kebabs are cooking, strain the marinade through a fine sieve into a small, heavy-bottomed saucepan. Heat the marinade through very gently, stirring occasionally; do not boil. Serve the kebabs garnished with lime wedges or slices and pass the heated marinade sauce separately.

SUGGESTED ACCOMPANIMENTS: *saffron rice; tomato and onion salad.*

Roulades Stuffed with Watercress and Walnuts

Serves 8
Working (and total) time: about 40 minutes

Calories **190**
Protein **22g**
Cholesterol **60mg**
Total fat **11g**
Saturated fat **2g**
Sodium **145mg**

1 kg	rump steak , about 2.5 cm (1 inch) thick, trimmed of fat	2 lb
2	bunches watercress, washed and stemmed	2
500 g	fresh spinach, washed and stemmed	1 lb
1 tbsp	olive oil	1 tbsp
30 g	walnuts, finely chopped	1 oz
1 tbsp	finely chopped fresh rosemary, or 1½ tsp dried rosemary	1 tbsp
2	anchovies, rinsed, patted dry and finely chopped	2
¼ tsp	salt	¼ tsp
	freshly ground black pepper	

Cut the steak in half across its width. Then, holding your knife blade parallel to the work surface, slice through both halves horizontally to form eight 5 cm (¼ inch) thick slices. (Alternatively, ask your butcher to slice the meat for you.)

Place a slice of beef between two sheets of plastic film and flatten it to 3 mm (⅛ inch) thickness by pounding first one side and then the other with a meat bat or the flat of a heavy knife. Flatten the remaining seven pieces in the same manner. Set the beef aside while you prepare the stuffing.

Bring 2 litres (3½ pints) of water to the boil in a large pan. Plunge the watercress into the boiling water and cook it for 30 seconds. Add the spinach, stir well, and cook the greens for 15 seconds longer. Drain the spinach and watercress, and squeeze them firmly into a ball to extract as much moisture as possible. Finely chop the ball of greens.

Heat ½ tablespoon of the oil in a heavy frying pan over medium heat. Add the walnuts, rosemary and anchovies. Cook the mixture, stirring, for 1 minute. Stir in the greens, salt and some pepper. Remove the pan from the heat.

Preheat the oven to 220°C (425°F or Mark 7). Spread 2 tablespoons of the stuffing on each piece of meat, leaving a 5 mm (¼ inch) border around the edges. Roll up the pieces, starting at a long edge, and set the roulades seam side down in a baking pan at least 2.5 cm (1 inch) apart.

Brush the roulades with the remaining oil. Bake them for 15 minutes. Remove the pan from the oven and allow the meat to stand for 5 minutes. Cut each roulade on the diagonal into six to eight thin slices.

SUGGESTED ACCOMPANIMENT: *steamed baby turnips.*

Roast Sirloin of Beef with Yorkshire Pudding

ROASTING A LEAN JOINT IN A ROASTING BAG ENSURES A MOIST, SUCCULENT RESULT. YORKSHIRE PUDDINGS MADE WITH OLIVE OIL INSTEAD OF DRIPPING AND WITH A MIXTURE OF MILK AND WATER ARE LIGHT AND FLUFFY — AND LOW IN SATURATED FAT.

Serves 6
Working time: about 30 minutes
Total time: about 1¼ hours

Calories **345**
Protein **40g**
Cholesterol **115mg**
Total fat **15g**
Saturated fat **5g**
Sodium **133mg**

1 kg	beef sirloin, boned, trimmed of fat, rolled and tied	2 to 2¼ lb
1 tbsp	grated fresh horseradish	1 tbsp
2 tsp	grainy mustard	2 tsp
4 tsp	plain flour	4 tsp
30 cl	brown stock (recipe, page 138)	½ pint
Yorkshire puddings		
60 g	plain flour	2 oz
⅛ tsp	salt	⅛ tsp
	freshly ground black pepper	
1	egg, beaten	1
12.5 cl	semi-skimmed milk	4 fl oz
1½ tbsp	virgin olive oil	1½ tbsp

Preheat the oven to 190°C (375°F or Mark 5). Mix together the horseradish and mustard, and brush over the top of the joint. Dust the inside of a roasting bag with 1 teaspoon of the flour (this helps to prevent spluttering during cooking), then place the joint in the bag with the horseradish mixture uppermost. Seal the bag according to the manufacturer's instructions, leaving an opening for steam to escape.

Place the bag in a roasting pan, making sure the opening in the bag faces uppermost so that the cooking juices do not run out. Allow 15 minutes roasting time per 500 g (1 lb) for rare meat, 20 minutes for medium and 25 minutes for well done.

Meanwhile, make the batter for the Yorkshire puddings. Sift the flour, salt and some pepper into a bowl, make a well in the centre and add the egg. In a measuring jug, make up the milk to 15 cl (¼ pint) with cold water, then gradually whisk it into the flour and egg. Beat well to remove any lumps. Cover the bowl and set aside until ready to cook.

Remove the joint from the oven but leave it in the bag. Increase the oven temperature to 220°C (425°F or Mark 7). Brush the olive oil over the inside of 12 patty tins and place them in the hottest part of the oven until smoking hot — 3 to 5 minutes. Remove the tins from the oven, whisk the batter and pour it into the tins. Return to the hottest part of the oven and cook for 15 to 20 minutes or until golden and well risen. Do not open the oven door during this time or the puddings will collapse.

While the Yorkshire puddings are cooking, remove the joint from the bag on to a heated platter and keep warm. Pour the cooking juices into a saucepan, add the stock and bring to the boil. Mix the remaining 3 teaspoons of flour with 1 tablespoon of cold water, add a few spoonfuls of the hot stock, then stir into the pan. Simmer, stirring, until the gravy reduces and thickens — about 5 minutes. Pour into a gravy boat.

When the Yorkshire puddings are ready, arrange them round the beef or pile them up on a warmed serving dish. Carve the meat at the table and pass the gravy separately.

SUGGESTED ACCOMPANIMENT: *French beans or cauliflower.*

Beef Fillet and Potato Roast

Serves 4
Working time: about 20 minutes
Total time: about 1 hour and 10 minutes

Calories **290**
Protein **27g**
Cholesterol **75mg**
Total fat **9g**
Saturated fat **3g**
Sodium **145mg**

600 g	beef fillet, trimmed of fat and cut into eight slices	1¼ lb
½ tsp	ground allspice	½ tsp
4 tbsp	chopped parsley	4 tbsp
1 tbsp	red wine vinegar	1 tbsp
⅛ tsp	salt	⅛ tsp
500 g	potatoes, scrubbed and cut into 5 mm (¼ inch) thick slices	1 lb
2	onions, thinly sliced	2
12.5 cl	unsalted brown or chicken stock (recipes, page 138)	4 fl oz

Preheat the oven to 180°C (350°F or Mark 4).

Mix the allspice, 2 tablespoons of the parsley, the vinegar and the salt in a small bowl. With your fingers, rub this mixture into the beef pieces and place them in a shallow dish. Let the meat marinate at room temperature while you make the potato gratin.

Combine the potatoes and onions in a fireproof baking dish. Pour in the stock and ¼ litre (8 fl oz) of water. Bring the liquid to the boil over medium-high heat, then bake the potatoes in the oven until they are tender and have browned — about 45 minutes. (If you do not have a fireproof baking dish, bring the potatoes, onions, stock and water to the boil in a saucepan, then transfer the mixture to a baking dish, and proceed as above.)

When the potatoes are cooked, remove the dish from the oven and increase the temperature to 230°C (450°F or Mark 8).

Heat a non-stick frying pan over medium-high heat. Pat the beef slices dry with a paper towel and sear them for 30 seconds on each side. Set the beef on top of the potatoes and return the dish to the oven. Bake the beef and potatoes for 3 minutes; turn the meat and bake it for 3 minutes more.

Sprinkle the remaining 2 tablespoons of parsley over the top before serving the roast.

SUGGESTED ACCOMPANIMENT: *steamed Brussels sprouts.*

Layered Meat Loaf

Serves 8
Working time: about 40 minutes
Total time: about 2 hours

Calories **220**
Protein **23g**
Cholesterol **55mg**
Total fat **8g**
Saturated fat **3g**
Sodium **230mg**

850 g	topside of beef, trimmed of fat and minced (box, page 15)	1¾ lb
500 g	ripe tomatoes, skinned, seeded and chopped	1 lb
1	onion, chopped	1
3	garlic cloves, finely chopped	3
1½ tsp	chopped fresh oregano, or ½ tsp dried oregano	1½ tsp
12.5 cl	port or Madeira	4 fl oz
2 tbsp	red wine vinegar	2 tbsp
1 tbsp	sugar	1 tbsp
¼ tsp	salt	¼ tsp
	freshly ground black pepper	
6 tbsp	freshly grated Parmesan cheese	6 tbsp
60 g	dry breadcrumbs	2 oz
1	egg white	1
1 tbsp	safflower oil	1 tbsp
2	bunches watercress, trimmed and washed	2
1 tbsp	fresh thyme, or 1 tsp dried thyme	1 tbsp

Heat a large, heavy frying pan over medium-high heat. Put in the tomatoes, onion, garlic and oregano. Cook, stirring occasionally, for 5 minutes. Add the port or Madeira, vinegar, sugar, ⅛ teaspoon of the salt and some pepper. Cook the mixture until almost all of the liquid has evaporated — about 10 minutes. Purée the mixture and place all but 4 tablespoons of it in a large bowl. Preheat the oven to 200°C (400°F or Mark 6).

Add the beef, 4 tablespoons of the grated cheese, half of the breadcrumbs, the remaining ⅛ teaspoon of salt, some pepper and the egg white to the tomato mixture in the bowl. Mix the ingredients well and set the meat aside while you prepare the watercress.

Heat the oil in a large, heavy frying pan over high heat. Add the watercress, thyme and some pepper. Cook, stirring constantly, until the watercress has wilted and almost all of the liquid has evaporated — 3 to 4 minutes. Chop the watercress finely. Place it in a bowl and combine it with the remaining breadcrumbs.

To layer the meat loaf, divide the beef mixture into three equal portions. Using a rolling pin or your hands, flatten each portion into a rectangle 12.5 cm (5 inches) wide, 20 cm (8 inches) long and 2 cm (¾ inch) thick.

Place one rectangle in a shallow baking pan. Top it with half of the watercress mixture, spreading the watercress evenly over the surface. Lay another rectangle on top and cover it with the remaining watercress. Finish with the final rectangle, then spread the reserved tomato sauce over the top and sides of the loaf. Sprinkle on the remaining 2 tablespoons of Parmesan cheese and bake the meat loaf for 1 hour and 10 minutes. Let the meat loaf stand for 10 minutes, then carefully transfer it to a platter, slice it and serve.

SUGGESTED ACCOMPANIMENT: *boiled new potatoes.*

Roast Beef with Root Vegetables

Serves 8
Working time: about 20 minutes
Total time: about 2 hours

Calories **205**
Protein **24g**
Cholesterol **60mg**
Total fat **7g**
Saturated fat **2g**
Sodium **165mg**

1 to 1.1 kg	rolled topside of beef or top rump, trimmed of fat	2¼ lb
1 tsp	safflower oil	1 tsp
¼ tsp	salt	¼ tsp
½ tsp	cracked black peppercorns	½ tsp
1	garlic clove, finely chopped	1
2	large carrots, peeled and sliced into 2 cm (¾ inch) rounds	2
2	large turnips, peeled and cut into 1 cm (½ inch) wedges	2
1	swede, peeled and cut into 2 cm (¾ inch) cubes	1
250 g	small white onions	8 oz
½ tbsp	fresh thyme, or ¾ tsp dried thyme	½ tbsp
4 tsp	cornflour	4 tsp
4 tbsp	semi-skimmed milk	4 tbsp
2 tsp	grainy mustard	2 tsp

Preheat the oven to 170°C (325°F or Mark 3).

Heat a large, non-stick frying pan over medium-high heat. Add the oil, tilting the pan to coat the bottom. Sear the roast in the pan — approximately 1 minute on each side.

Transfer the meat to a roasting pan, sprinkle the meat with the salt, peppercorns and garlic, and roast the beef until it is medium rare and registers 60°C (140°F) on a meat thermometer — about 1¼ hours. Remove the roast from the pan and set it aside. Skim and discard any fat from the juices in the pan; set the pan with its juices aside.

Toss the carrots, turnips, swede and onions with the thyme. Pour enough water into a large pan to fill it 2.5 cm (1 inch) deep. Place a vegetable steamer in the pan and bring the water to the boil. Put the vegetables into the steamer, cover the pan, and cook the vegetables until they are tender — about 10 minutes. Remove the vegetables from the steamer and keep them warm.

Pour about ¼ litre (8 fl oz) of the steaming liquid into the roasting pan. Simmer the liquid over medium-high heat, stirring constantly to dissolve any caramelized roasting juices on the bottom of the pan. Mix the cornflour and milk in a small bowl, then whisk this mixture into the simmering liquid. Stir the liquid until the sauce thickens, then whisk in the mustard. Remove the pan from the heat and keep it warm.

Slice the roast and arrange the slices on a platter. Toss the vegetables with some of the sauce and place them around the meat. Serve the roast with the remaining sauce passed separately.

SUGGESTED ACCOMPANIMENT: *steamed kale or spinach.*

Spicy Beef Salad

Serves 4
Working time: about 25 minutes
Total time: about 2 hours and 45 minutes
(includes marinating)

Calories **295**
Protein **22g**
Cholesterol **55mg**
Total fat **5g**
Saturated fat **2g**
Sodium **120mg**

500 g	sirloin steak in one piece, trimmed of fat	1 lb
8	whole cloves	8
8	black peppercorns	8
12	allspice berries	12
1	large onion, thinly sliced	1
2 tbsp	brandy	2 tbsp
½ litre	red wine	16 fl oz
175 g	mixed dried fruit, coarsely chopped	6 oz
4 tbsp	red wine vinegar	4 tbsp
1	cinnamon stick	1
500 g	turnips, peeled, halved lengthwise and sliced	1 lb
4 tbsp	chopped parsley	4 tbsp
	several watercress sprigs (optional), trimmed, washed and dried	

Put the steak into a shallow pan with the cloves, peppercorns, allspice berries, onion slices, brandy and ¼ litre (8 fl oz) of the wine. Let the steak marinate at room temperature for 2 hours, turning it every now and then.

In a saucepan, combine the dried fruit with the vinegar, the remaining wine, ¼ litre (8 fl oz) of water and the cinnamon stick. Bring the liquid to the boil, then lower the heat, and simmer the mixture for 30 minutes. Drain the fruit in a sieve set over a bowl; discard the cinnamon stick and set the fruit aside. Return the liquid to the saucepan and boil it until it is reduced by about half — approximately 5 minutes.

Preheat the oven to 240°C (475°F or Mark 9).

Pour enough water into a saucepan to fill it about 2.5 cm (1 inch) deep. Set a vegetable steamer in the pan and bring the water to the boil. Put the turnips into the steamer, cover the pan, and steam the turnips until they are tender — about 10 minutes. Transfer the turnips to a bowl and set them aside.

Remove the steak from the marinade and pat it dry with paper towels; discard the marinade. Roast the steak for 15 minutes, then remove it from the oven, and let it rest for 30 minutes. Cut the steak against the grain into slices about 5 mm (¼ inch) thick. Cut each slice into strips about 4 cm (1½ inches) long.

Toss the strips of beef with the reduced wine mixture, parsley, turnips and the reserved fruit. Arrange the salad on a platter; garnish it with watercress, if you like, and serve.

SUGGESTED ACCOMPANIMENT: *small wholemeal rolls.*

Skewered Meatballs with Aubergine Relish

Serves 8
Working time: about 1 hour
Total time: about 1 hour and 30 minutes

Calories **235**
Protein **26g**
Cholesterol **60mg**
Total fat **7g**
Saturated fat **2g**
Sodium **190mg**

1.1 kg	topside of beef, trimmed of fat and minced (box, page 15)	2¼ lb
1 kg	aubergines, pierced in several places with a knife	2 lb
2	onions, finely chopped	2
6	garlic cloves, finely chopped	6
1 tsp	olive oil	1 tsp
4 tbsp	chopped fresh mint, or 2 tsp dried oregano	4 tbsp
3 tbsp	fresh lemon juice	3 tbsp
¼ tsp	salt	¼ tsp
	freshly ground black pepper	
4	slices wholemeal bread	4
5 tbsp	chopped parsley	5 tbsp
12.5 cl	plain low-fat yogurt	4 fl oz
	several mint sprigs (optional)	

Preheat the oven to 240°C (475°F or Mark 9).

Roast the aubergines in the oven, turning them occasionally, until they are blistered on all sides — about 20 minutes. Transfer the aubergines to a bowl, cover it with plastic film and refrigerate it. ▶

Simmer the onion, garlic, oil and 4 tablespoons of water in a heavy saucepan until the onion is translucent — about 5 minutes. Increase the heat and boil the mixture until the water has evaporated — approximately 1 minute.

To prepare the relish, peel the skin from the aubergines and purée the flesh in a blender or a food processor. Remove 4 tablespoons of the aubergine purée and set it aside. In a small bowl, combine the rest of the aubergine with the chopped mint or dried oregano, lemon juice, half of the onion and garlic mixture, 1/8 teaspoon of the salt and a generous grinding of pepper. Put the aubergine relish into the refrigerator.

Soak the bread slices for 3 minutes in enough water to cover them. Using your hands, gently squeeze the water from the bread.

Mix the minced beef, moist bread, parsley, the rest of the onion and garlic mixture, the reserved aubergine purée, the remaining salt and a generous grinding of black pepper. Form the meat mixture into 48 meatballs. Thread three meatballs on each of 16 skewers and set them on a baking sheet. Cook the meatballs in the oven until they are browned — 10 to 15 minutes.

Arrange the meatballs on a platter and, if you like, garnish the dish with sprigs of mint. Pass the aubergine relish and the yogurt separately.

SUGGESTED ACCOMPANIMENT: *pitta bread.*

Mediterranean Meat Loaf

Serves 10
Working time: about 1 hour
Total time: about 2 hours

Calories **220**
Protein **22g**
Cholesterol **50mg**
Total fat **6g**
Saturated fat **2g**
Sodium **140mg**

1 to 1.1 kg	topside of beef, trimmed of fat and minced (box, page 15)	2¼ lb
1 tsp	olive oil	1 tsp
2	carrots, finely chopped	2
2	sticks celery, finely chopped	2
2	onions, finely chopped	2
500 g	aubergine, finely chopped	1 lb
1	sweet red pepper, seeded, deribbed and finely chopped	1
1	sweet green pepper, seeded, deribbed and finely chopped	1
8	garlic cloves, finely chopped	8
6	large ripe tomatoes, skinned, seeded and chopped, or 800 g (28 oz) canned whole tomatoes, crushed and drained	6
4 tbsp	finely chopped fresh oregano, or 4 tsp dried oregano	4 tbsp
135 g	fresh breadcrumbs	4½ oz
2 tbsp	currants (optional)	2 tbsp
20	preserved vine leaves (optional), stemmed, rinsed and patted dry	20

Heat a large, non-stick frying pan over medium heat. Add the oil, carrots, celery, onions, aubergine, peppers and garlic. Cook the mixture, stirring frequently, until the vegetables are soft — about 8 minutes.

Add the tomatoes and oregano to the pan. Increase the heat to medium high and bring the liquid to a simmer, then simmer the tomatoes for 2 minutes. Remove half the mixture and set it aside.

Continue cooking the mixture remaining in the pan until the liquid has evaporated — about 10 minutes. Scrape the vegetables into a large bowl and let them cool slightly. Add the beef, the breadcrumbs and the currants, if you are using them. Knead the mixture with your hands to incorporate the ingredients.

Preheat the oven to 180°C (350°F or Mark 4).

Line a 3 litre (5 pint) ring mould with the vine leaves if you are using them — this adds a special effect.

Spoon the meat mixture into the mould, patting it down to release trapped air. Trim any protruding vine leaves.

Bake the loaf for 1 hour. After about 50 minutes, reheat the reserved vegetable mixture over medium heat. Invert a serving plate on top of the mould; turn both over, then gently lift off the mould. Fill the space in the centre of the meat loaf with some of the hot vegetables and spoon the rest into a bowl.

SUGGESTED ACCOMPANIMENT: *orzo or other small pasta shapes.*

Roast Fillet of Beef with Spinach Sauce and Almonds

Serves 6
Working time: about 20 minutes
Total time: about 1 hour

Calories **230**
Protein **22g**
Cholesterol **65mg**
Total fat **13g**
Saturated fat **3g**
Sodium **165mg**

850 g	beef fillet in one piece, trimmed of fat	1¾ lb
4 tsp	safflower oil	4 tsp
¼ tsp	salt	¼ tsp
	freshly ground black pepper	
2 tbsp	slivered almonds	2 tbsp
3 tbsp	finely chopped shallot	3 tbsp
¼ litre	dry white wine	8 fl oz
250 g	fresh spinach, stemmed and washed	8 oz
4 tbsp	skimmed milk	4 tbsp
⅛ tsp	grated nutmeg	⅛ tsp

Preheat the oven to 170°C (325°F or Mark 3).

Heat 1 teaspoon of the oil in a large, non-stick frying pan over high heat. Sear the meat in the pan until it is browned on all sides — 2 to 3 minutes in all. Season the fillet with ⅛ teaspoon of the salt and a liberal grinding of pepper. Transfer the fillet to a roasting pan; do not wash the frying pan. Finish cooking the meat in the oven — about 35 minutes, or until a meat thermometer inserted in the centre registers 60°C (140°F) for medium-rare meat.

Heat a small, heavy frying pan over medium heat. Add the slivered almonds and toast them, stirring constantly, until they are lightly browned — 2 to 3 minutes. Remove the toasted almonds from the pan and set them aside.

To make the sauce, heat the remaining oil in the large frying pan over medium heat. Add the shallot and cook it until it is translucent — about 2 minutes. Pour in the wine and simmer the liquid until about 6 tablespoons remain — 6 to 8 minutes.

Remove the fillet from the oven and let it rest for 10 minutes while you complete the sauce.

Add the spinach to the shallot-wine mixture and reduce the heat to low. Cover the pan and cook the spinach until it has wilted — 1 to 2 minutes. Stir in the milk and nutmeg. Return the mixture to a simmer, then transfer it to a blender or a food processor, and purée it. Season the sauce with the remaining salt and some freshly ground pepper.

Carve the beef into 12 slices and arrange them on a warmed serving platter. Spoon some of the sauce over the slices and sprinkle them with the almonds. Pass the remaining sauce separately.

SUGGESTED ACCOMPANIMENT: *steamed julienned carrots.*

Roast Sirloin with Mushroom Sauce

Serves 10
Working time: about 30 minutes
Total time: about 1 hour

Calories **205**
Protein **21g**
Cholesterol **55mg**
Total fat **10g**
Saturated fat **3g**
Sodium **170mg**

1.25 kg	boned and rolled sirloin, trimmed of fat	2½ lb
4 tbsp	cracked black peppercorns	4 tbsp
2½ tbsp	Dijon mustard	2½ tbsp
2 tbsp	plain low-fat yogurt	2 tbsp
2 tbsp	olive oil	2 tbsp
250 g	mushrooms, wiped clean and quartered	8 oz
40 g	shallots, thinly sliced	1½ oz
1 tbsp	chopped fresh rosemary, or ¾ tsp dried rosemary	1 tbsp
¼ litre	red wine	8 fl oz
1	garlic clove, finely chopped	1
½ litre	unsalted brown or chicken stock, (recipes, page 138)	16 fl oz
¼ tsp	salt	¼ tsp
4 tbsp	double cream, mixed with 1 tbsp cornflour	4 tbsp

Preheat the oven to 240°C (475°F or Mark 9).

Spread the cracked peppercorns on a plate. Mix 2 tablespoons of the mustard with the yogurt and smear this mixture over the beef. Roll the beef in the peppercorns, coating it evenly on all sides. Place the beef on a rack set in a roasting pan. For medium-rare meat, cook the roast until a meat thermometer inserted in the centre registers 60°C (140°F) — about 35 minutes. Let the roast stand while you prepare the mushroom sauce.

Heat the oil in a large, heavy frying pan over medium heat. Add the mushrooms, shallots and rosemary, and cook them, stirring often, for 5 minutes. Add the wine and garlic, then rapidly boil the liquid until it is reduced by half — about 3 minutes. Stir in the stock and salt; reduce the sauce once again until only about 30 cl (½ pint) of liquid remains. Whisk in the cream-and-cornflour mixture along with the remaining ½ tablespoon of mustard; simmer the sauce for 1 minute more to thicken it.

To serve, carve the roast into 20 very thin slices. Arrange the slices on a serving platter and pour the mushroom sauce over them.

SUGGESTED ACCOMPANIMENT: *steamed broccoli florets.*

Roast Fillet of Beef with Spinach and Sprouts

Serves 8
Working time: about 30 minutes
Total time: about 2 hours (includes marinating)

Calories **240**
Protein **27g**
Cholesterol **75mg**
Total fat **12g**
Saturated fat **4g**
Sodium **160mg**

1.25 kg	beef fillet in one piece, trimmed of fat	2 ½ lb
2 tbsp	toasted sesame seeds	2 tbsp
4 tbsp	low-sodium soy sauce or shoyu	4 tbsp
3 tbsp	rice vinegar or white wine vinegar	3 tbsp
1 tbsp	dark brown sugar	1 tbsp
1 tbsp	safflower oil	1 tbsp
350 g	fresh spinach, washed, stemmed and sliced into 5 mm (¼ inch) wide strips	12 oz
2	large ripe tomatoes, skinned, seeded and sliced into 5 mm (¼ inch) wide strips	2
400 g	bean sprouts	14 oz

To make the marinade, purée 1 tablespoon of the sesame seeds, 3 tablespoons of the soy sauce, 2 tablespoons of the vinegar, and the brown sugar in a blender. Put the fillet into a shallow dish, then pour the marinade over it, and let it stand for 1 hour at room temperature, turning the meat occasionally.

Preheat the oven to 170°C (325°F or Mark 3). Drain the fillet, discarding the marinade, and pat it dry with paper towels. Pour the oil into a large, shallow fireproof casserole set over high heat. When the oil is hot, sear the meat until it is well browned on all sides — 3 to 5 minutes. Place the casserole in the oven. For medium-rare meat, roast the beef for 40 to 45 minutes or until a meat thermometer inserted in the centre registers 60°C (140°F). Remove the meat from the oven and let it rest while you prepare the garnish.

Heat a large frying pan or wok over medium heat. Add the spinach strips and cook them, stirring constantly, until their liquid has evaporated — 2 to 3 minutes. Stir in the tomato strips and the bean sprouts, and cook the vegetables until they are heated through — 3 to 4 minutes more. Remove the pan from the heat and stir in the remaining soy sauce and the remaining vinegar.

Cut the beef into 16 slices and arrange them on a platter. Surround the beef slices with the spinach-and-sprout garnish. Sprinkle the remaining tablespoon of sesame seeds over the garnish and serve.

SUGGESTED ACCOMPANIMENT: *boiled potatoes tossed with finely chopped spring onion greens.*

Beef Fillet with Basil and Sun-Dried Tomatoes

Serves 4
Working time: about 35 minutes
Total time: about 2 hours

Calories **340**
Protein **28g**
Cholesterol **75mg**
Total fat **17g**
Saturated fat **4g**
Sodium **415mg**

600 g	beef fillet in one piece, trimmed of fat	1¼ lb
45 g	fresh basil leaves, thinly sliced	1½ oz
4 tbsp	sun-dried tomatoes packed in oil, drained and finely chopped	4 tbsp
1 tsp	safflower oil	1 tsp
Stuffed cherry tomatoes		
2	whole garlic bulbs, cloves separated but not peeled	2
45 g	fresh basil leaves	1½ oz
⅛ tsp	salt	⅛ tsp
	freshly ground black pepper	
1 tsp	fresh lemon juice	1 tsp
4 tbsp	plain low-fat yogurt	4 tbsp
24	cherry tomatoes	24

Preheat the oven to 170°C (325°F or Mark 3).

Using a well-scrubbed sharpening steel or some other thick, pointed tool, pierce the beef fillet through the centre; rotate the sharpening steel so as to ceate a 1 cm (½ inch) wide hole.

Combine the thinly sliced basil leaves with the sun-dried tomatoes. Using your fingers, fill the hole with the basil-tomato mixture.

Heat the oil in a heavy, shallow fireproof casserole

over high heat. When the oil is hot, sear the fillet until it is well browned on all sides — 3 to 5 minutes. Transfer the casserole to the oven. For medium-rare meat, roast the beef for 25 to 30 minutes or until a thermometer inserted in the meat registers 60°C (140°F). Remove the fillet from the oven and let it rest until it is cool — about 45 minutes.

Meanwhile, prepare the filling for the cherry tomatoes. Put the garlic cloves into a small saucepan and pour in just enough water to cover them. Bring the water to the boil, then reduce the heat, and simmer the cloves until they are very soft — 30 to 45 minutes. Drain the garlic; when the cloves are cool enough to

handle, squeeze the pulp from the skins into a blender or a food processor. Add the unsliced basil leaves, the salt, some pepper, the lemon juice and the yogurt, and purée the mixture. Set the purée aside.

Cut the tops off the cherry tomatoes. With a melon baller or a small spoon, scoop out the seeds. Using a piping bag or a spoon, fill the tomatoes with the purée.

Carve the beef into 5 mm (¼ inch) thick slices and transfer them to plates or a platter. Arrange the filled tomatoes around the slices of beef and serve the meat at room temperature.

SUGGESTED ACCOMPANIMENT: *wholemeal rolls.*

Roast Beef with Cloves and Red Peppers

Serves 12
Working time: about 30 minutes
Total time: about 2 hours

Calories **180**	1.75 kg	rolled topside of beef or top rump, trimmed of fat	3½ lb
Protein **23g**	4	sweet red peppers	4
Cholesterol **65mg**	1 tsp	ground cloves	1 tsp
Total fat **7g**	1 tbsp	safflower oil	1 tbsp
Saturated fat **2g**	½ tsp	salt	½ tsp
Sodium **155mg**		freshly ground black pepper	
	¼ litre	unsalted brown or chicken stock (recipes, page 138)	8 fl oz
	500 g	white onions	1 lb
	12.5 cl	dry white wine	4 fl oz

Roast the peppers about 5 cm (2 inches) below a preheated grill, turning them as they blister, until they are blackened on all sides — about 15 minutes in all. Transfer the peppers to a bowl and cover it with plastic film; the trapped steam will loosen their skins. Set the bowl aside.

Preheat the oven to 140°C (275°F or Mark 1). Sprinkle the meat all over with ½ teaspoon of the cloves.

Heat the oil in a large, heavy frying pan over high heat. When it is hot, add the beef and sear it until it is well browned on all sides — about 5 minutes. Transfer the beef to a shallow fireproof casserole and sprinkle it with ¼ teaspoon of the salt and a generous grinding of pepper.

Roast the beef for 1 hour. If the meat juices begin to blacken in the bottom of the casserole, pour in a few tablespoons of the stock.

While the joint is roasting, peel the peppers, working over a bowl to catch the juice. Strain the juice and set aside. Slice the peppers into strips about 2.5 cm (1 inch) long and 1 cm (½ inch) wide. Cut the onions in half from top to bottom, then slice them with the grain

into strips roughly the same size as the pepper strips.

When the joint has cooked for 1 hour, add to the casserole the peppers and their juice, the onions, the stock, the wine, the remaining ground cloves and the remaining salt. For medium-rare meat, roast the beef for 30 minutes longer, or until a meat thermometer inserted into the centre registers 60°C (140°F).

Remove the casserole from the oven and set the roast aside while you finish the dish.

With a slotted spoon, transfer the vegetables to a bowl. Boil the liquid remaining in the casserole until it is reduced to about 12.5 cl (4 fl oz). Cut the meat into very thin slices and arrange them on a platter with the vegetables surrounding them. Dribble the sauce over the beef and serve immediately.

SUGGESTED ACCOMPANIMENT: *roasted sweet potatoes.*

Mushroom-Stuffed Roast Beef

Serves 8
Working time: about 45 minutes
Total time: about 2 hours

Calories **190**
Protein **26g**
Cholesterol **65mg**
Total fat **7g**
Saturated fat **3g**
Sodium **200mg**

1.25 kg	corner piece of topside of beef, trimmed of fat	2½ lb
250 g	fresh shiitake mushrooms, wiped clean, caps finely chopped, stems reserved	8 oz
250 g	mushrooms, wiped clean, caps finely chopped, stems reserved	8 oz
60 cl	dry white wine	1 pint
12.5 cl	Madeira or port	4 fl oz
8	spring onions, white parts finely chopped, green parts reserved	8
3	lemons, grated rind only	3
½ tsp	salt	½ tsp
	freshly ground black pepper	
4 tbsp	toasted breadcrumbs	4 tbsp

Preheat the oven to 200°C (400°F or Mark 6).

Combine the mushrooms, ½ litre (16 fl oz) of the white wine, and the Madeira or port in a large, non-reactive frying pan. Bring the liquid to the boil over medium-high heat, then continue cooking it until all the liquid has evaporated — about 15 minutes. Transfer the mushrooms to a bowl and mix in the chopped spring onions, lemon rind, salt and some pepper. Set the mixture aside.

Using the techniques shown below, cut the joint and stuff it. Put the joint into a roasting pan and cover the exposed mushroom mixture with the breadcrumbs. Scatter the reserved mushroom stems and spring onions around the meat and roast it for 30 minutes.

Pour the remaining white wine over the joint and continue roasting the beef for 15 minutes for medium-rare meat. (The internal temperature should be 60°C/

140°F.) Transfer the joint to a carving board and allow it to rest for 15 minutes.

Heat the juices in the roasting pan over medium heat, scraping up any caramelized juices with a wooden spoon to dissolve them. Skim off the fat, strain the juices and keep them warm.

Carve the beef into eight slices and serve them with the juices spooned on top.

SUGGESTED ACCOMPANIMENT: *steamed spinach.*

EDITOR'S NOTE: *If fresh shiitake mushrooms are unavailable, ordinary cultivated mushrooms may be substituted.*

Stuffing a Topside Roast

1 *TRIMMING THE FAT IN STRIPS. With a small, thin-bladed knife (here, a boning knife), cut into the fatty layer of the joint to form a tab. Pull the tab taut, and insert the knife under it. Carefully slide the knife towards you to remove a strip of fat. Continue cutting off strips until the entire layer of fat is removed.*

2 *MAKING THE FIRST SLICE. Steadying the joint with one hand, place a slicing knife along the meat's edge, about one third of the way down from the surface. With a smooth sawing motion, cut across the meat, stopping just short of the edge so that the flaps remain attached.*

3 *MAKING THE SECOND SLICE. Rotate the meat on the work surface and unfold the thinner flap from the thicker one. Now cut through the inside edge of the thicker flap, again leaving a small hinge of meat to keep the pieces connected.*

4 *STUFFING THE BEEF. Unfold the newly formed flap. You will have three joined squares of meat. Spread one third of the stuffing on to the middle square and fold the left flap over it. Spread half of the remaining stuffing on top (above). Fold the right flap over the stuffing and cover the flap with the rest of the stuffing.*

French Roast Veal with Grapefruit and Herbs

COOKING LARGE PIECES OF MEAT AND WHOLE BIRDS IN A
SMALL AMOUNT OF LIQUID IS CALLED "FRENCH ROASTING"
AND IS A GOOD WAY TO ROAST LEAN MEATS TO ENSURE
SUCCULENCE. WHEN ROASTED WITHOUT LIQUID, LEAN CUTS
TEND TO TOUGHEN AND DRY OUT.

Serves 6
Working time: about 40 minutes
Total time: about 2 hours and 20 minutes

Calories **250**
Protein **15g**
Cholesterol **120mg**
Total fat **13g**
Saturated fat **5g**
Sodium **155mg**

1.25 to 1.5 kg	loin of veal, boned and trimmed of fat	2½ to 3 lb
3	grapefruits	3
1	garlic clove, crushed	1
2 tbsp	light grainy mustard	2 tbsp
2 tsp	chopped fresh rosemary, or 1 tsp dried rosemary, crumbled	2 tsp
2 tsp	chopped fresh thyme, or ½ tsp dried thyme	2 tsp
	freshly ground black pepper	
1 tbsp	virgin olive oil	1 tbsp
20 cl	unsalted chicken or veal stock (recipes, page 138)	7 fl oz
1	bouquet garni (parsley, thyme, bay leaf)	1
⅛ tsp	salt	⅛ tsp
	fresh rosemary and thyme sprigs for garnish (optional)	

Preheat the oven to 180°C (350°F or Mark 4). Finely
grate the rind of two of the grapefruits into a bowl.
Add the garlic, then half each of the mustard, chopped
rosemary, thyme and some pepper. Mix well, then
spread over the inside (boned-out part) of the veal. Roll
up the joint and tie securely at regular intervals with
string. Spread the remaining mustard over the outside
of the rolled-up joint.

Halve one of the three grapefruits and squeeze the
juice. Heat the oil in a large fireproof casserole over
high heat and sear the veal on all sides, turning it
frequently — about 10 minutes in all. Pour the fruit
juice and the stock over the veal and bring to the boil.
Add the bouquet garni, salt and some pepper. Transfer
the casserole to the oven and roast, uncovered, for 1½
hours, turning the veal over every 20 minutes or so and
basting with the cooking juices. The meat is ready if the
juices run clear when a skewer is inserted in the centre
of the joint — or the internal temperature reading is
75°C (165°F) on a meat thermometer. While the veal is
cooking, peel and segment the remaining two grapefruits for the garnish. Prepare the grapefruit segments over a bowl to catch the juice, and set both
segments and juice aside.

Transfer the veal to a warmed serving dish, cover
and keep hot. Place the casserole on top of the stove
and remove the bouquet garni. Add the grapefruit
juice from the garnish to the cooking juices and boil to
reduce slightly, stirring all the time — about 5
minutes. Remove from the heat and stir in the remaining chopped herbs.

Remove the string from the veal and carve the meat
into neat slices. Arrange on a platter or individual
plates with the grapefruit segments. Pour over a little
of the cooking juices and garnish with sprigs of rosemary and thyme, if desired. Pass the remaining cooking juices separately.

SUGGESTED ACCOMPANIMENT: *steamed broccoli and new
potatoes.*

EDITOR'S NOTE: *To give this dish added colour, use segments of
one pink and one yellow-fleshed grapefruit for the garnish.*

Peppered Veal Fillet

Serves 4
Working time: about 20 minutes
Total time: about 3 hours and 15 minutes
(includes marinating)

Calories **180**
Protein **40g**
Cholesterol **90mg**
Total fat **10g**
Saturated fat **2g**
Sodium **185mg**

500 g	veal fillet, trimmed of fat	1 lb
30 g	pumpkin seeds	1 oz
1 tsp	dried green peppercorns	1 tsp
½ tsp	black peppercorns	½ tsp
¼ tsp	hot red pepper flakes	¼ tsp
1 tsp	Dijon mustard	1 tsp
350 g	ripe tomatoes, skinned, seeded and chopped, or 200 g (7 oz) canned tomatoes, drained and chopped	12 oz
	watercress sprigs for garnish	

Toast the pumpkin seeds in a small, non-stick frying pan over medium heat, until golden-brown but not over-brown — stirring them with a long-handled spoon and standing well back because the seeds will snap and jump. Grind the toasted seeds finely in a blender or food processor.

Crush the green and black peppercorns and the pepper flakes finely in a mortar and pestle, then tip into a medium-sized bowl. Add the pumpkin seeds and the mustard, mix well, then add the tomatoes and bind to a wet paste. Place the veal fillet in the bowl and smear the paste all over it. Cover and marinate in the refrigerator for at least 2 hours.

Preheat the oven to 240°C (475°F or Mark 9).

Transfer the fillet to a small roasting pan and press on any pepper paste left in the bowl, checking that the ends are also covered. Roast for 10 minutes, then reduce the heat to 180°C (350°F or Mark 4) and continue roasting for 35 minutes longer. The veal should still be pink at this point; if you prefer the meat well done, roast for a further 10 to 15 minutes.

Remove the veal from the oven, cover loosely with foil and leave to rest in a warm place for 10 minutes. To serve, carve the veal into thick slices and garnish with watercress sprigs.

SUGGESTED ACCOMPANIMENT: *steamed, buttered pumpkin and mange-tout.*

Roast Loin and Sweetcorn-Watercress Pilaff

Serves 8
Working time: about 1 hour
Total time: about 2 hours and 15 minutes

Calories **275**
Protein **30g**
Cholesterol **110mg**
Total fat **14g**
Saturated fat **5g**
Sodium **220mg**

1 kg	boned loin of veal	2 lb
2 tsp	safflower oil	2 tsp
1	onion, finely chopped	1
1	stick celery, finely chopped	1
2 tbsp	semi-skimmed milk	2 tbsp
300 g	fresh sweetcorn kernels (about 4 ears), or 300 g (10 oz) frozen sweetcorn kernels, thawed and drained	10 oz
125 g	cooked brown rice	4 oz
60 g	watercress leaves, chopped	2 oz
½ tsp	salt	½ tsp
	freshly ground black pepper	
4 tbsp	medium sherry	4 tbsp

Trim excess fat from the loin of veal, being careful not to cut through the membranes that hold the joint together. Open out the joint on a work surface.

Preheat the oven to 180°C (350°F or Mark 4). Heat the oil in a small, non-stick frying pan over medium-low heat. Add the onion and celery and cook gently, stirring, until softened — about 5 minutes. Tip the vegetables into a bowl.

Put the milk in a food processor and add 30 g (1 oz) of the rice. Blend the milk and rice to a smooth paste, then turn the paste into a bowl.

Add the sweetcorn kernels to the onion and celery together with the watercress, salt and some pepper, and mix together. Add a quarter of this mixture to the rice paste and mix well. Spread the sweetcorn and rice paste over the surface of the loin of veal, then roll it up carefully and tie into a neat shape with string *(page 134, Step 3)*. Put the joint into a roasting bag and place the bag in a roasting pan.

Add the remaining rice to the rest of the sweetcorn mixture and spoon it into the roasting bag round the joint. Close the end of the bag with a plastic tie, and cut several slits in the bag. Roast for 1¼ to 1½ hours; test if the veal is cooked by piercing it with a skewer or the tip of a knife through one of the slits in the bag. The juices that run out of the meat should be only faintly pink, or clear.

Cut open the top of the roasting bag and lift the joint on to a carving dish. Use a slotted spoon to transfer the sweetcorn-watercress pilaff to the dish, draining it well and arranging it round the joint. Cover the meat and pilaff and set aside to rest in a warm place for 10 minutes.

Meanwhile, strain the cooking juices left in the roasting bag into a small saucepan. Add the sherry, bring to the boil and boil for 1 minute.

Carve the veal into thick slices on the bed of pilaff, and serve with the sherried juices.

SUGGESTED ACCOMPANIMENTS: *granary bread; carrots.*

Veal Chops with Artichokes

Serves 4
Working time: about 45 minutes
Total time: about 2 hours

Calories **280**
Protein **24g**
Cholesterol **120mg**
Total fat **17g**
Saturated fat **6g**
Sodium **315mg**

4	veal loin chops (about 250g/8 oz each), trimmed of fat	4
4 tbsp	lemon juice	4 tbsp
4	globe artichokes, thoroughly washed	4
1 tbsp	safflower oil	1 tbsp
4 tbsp	dry sherry	4 tbsp
1½ tbsp	chopped fresh tarragon or oregano, or 1 tsp dried oregano	1½ tbsp
½ tsp	salt	½ tsp
	freshly ground black pepper	
2 tbsp	double cream	2 tbsp

Bring about 2 litres (3½ pints) of water to the boil in a large, non-reactive pan. Add the lemon juice. Cut off the stems of the artichokes close to the base and place them bottom down in the boiling water (this will seal the cut surface and prevent it discolouring). Simmer the artichokes for about 30 minutes. To test if they are cooked, a knife inserted in an artichoke bottom should meet no resistance, and a leaf gently tugged should easily pull free. Drain the artichokes by putting them upside down in a colander.

Preheat the oven to 180°C (350°F or Mark 4).

When the artichokes are cool enough to handle, pull off the leaves until you reach the hairy choke; reserve the leaves and discard the choke, then trim the artichoke bottoms into neat rounds, reserving the trimmings. Cut the bottoms into 5 mm (¼ inch) cubes.

Heat the oil in a large, non-stick frying pan over high heat. Add the chops and brown them for 1 to 2 minutes on each side. Transfer the chops to a large sheet of foil placed over a baking sheet. Pile the diced artichoke bottoms on the chops, then sprinkle over the sherry, two thirds of the tarragon or fresh oregano (or all the dried oregano, if using), the salt and some pepper. Wrap the foil round the chops and seal it tightly. Put the chops in the oven and bake them for 30 minutes.

Meanwhile, using a table knife, scrape off the bottom part of each artichoke leaf and put it in a food processor or blender with the reserved trimmings.

Carefully transfer the chops to a serving platter and keep hot. To make the sauce, pour the cooking juices from the foil into the food processor or blender and blend the artichoke mixture. Pass the mixture through a fine sieve into a small saucepan and add the cream. Bring to the boil and boil for 1 minute. Spoon the sauce over the chops, sprinkle with the remaining tarragon or fresh oregano (or a little parsley, if dried oregano has been used) and serve immediately.

SUGGESTED ACCOMPANIMENTS: *jacket-baked potatoes; red onion and bulb fennel salad.*

Fillet Stuffed with Oranges and Black Olives

Serves 4
Working time: about 35 minutes
Total time: about 1 hour and 30 minutes

Calories **400**
Protein **30g**
Cholesterol **90mg**
Total fat **9g**
Saturated fat **2g**
Sodium **240mg**

500 g	veal fillet (in one piece), trimmed of fat	1 lb
3	oranges	3
6	black olives, stoned and chopped	6
60 g	fresh brown breadcrumbs	2 oz
1	egg white	1
	freshly ground black pepper	
2	garlic cloves, cut into thin slivers	2
1 tbsp	virgin olive oil	1 tbsp
1 tbsp	brandy	1 tbsp
2 tbsp	dry white wine	2 tbsp
17.5 cl	freshly squeezed orange juice	6 fl oz
3	bay leaves	3
	black olives for garnish	

Preheat the oven to 180°C (350°F or Mark 4). Grate the rinds of two of the oranges. Remove the peel and pith of all three oranges, then chop the flesh of one and slice the other two.

Cut a slit along one side of the veal to make a pocket in the centre. Put the orange rind and the chopped orange in a bowl and add the olives, breadcrumbs, egg white and some pepper. Stir well to mix. Pack the stuffing mixture into the pocket in the veal, close up the slit and tie the fillet neatly into shape with string *(page 135, Step 3)*. Make small incisions in the meat at regular intervals with the point of a sharp knife, then insert the garlic. Rub a little pepper all over the meat.

Heat the oil in a fireproof casserole over high heat. Add the veal and sear it on all sides — about 5 minutes. Remove the casserole and reduce the heat.

Warm the brandy gently in a ladle. Remove it from the heat, ignite it with a match and pour the flaming brandy over the veal. When the flames subside, pour over the wine and orange juice. Return the casserole to the heat and bring slowly to the boil. Add the bay leaves. Transfer the casserole to the oven and roast the veal, uncovered, for 50 minutes, turning the veal over and basting it with the cooking juices about every 15 minutes.

Transfer the meat to a warmed serving dish, cover and keep hot. Place the casserole on top of the stove and discard the bay leaves. Boil to reduce slightly, stirring all the time — 3 to 5 minutes.

Remove the string from the veal and carve the meat into neat slices. Arrange them in overlapping slices on a warmed serving platter, interleaving with the slices of orange. Pour over a little of the cooking juices and garnish with the olives. Serve immediately.

SUGGESTED ACCOMPANIMENT: *French beans.*

Veal Chops with Spinach and Ricotta

Serves 4
Working time: about 45 minutes
Total time: about 1 hour and 15 minutes

Calories **310** Protein **33g** Cholesterol **120mg** Total fat **17g** Saturated fat **5g** Sodium **290mg**	4	veal loin chops (about 250 g/8 oz each), trimmed of fat	4
	750 g	ripe tomatoes, skinned, seeded and chopped, or 400 g (14 oz) canned tomatoes, chopped	1½ lb
	2	large fresh rosemary sprigs, or 1 tsp dried rosemary, crumbled	2
	2 tbsp	virgin olive oil	2 tbsp
	1	onion, finely chopped	1
	125 g	fresh spinach leaves, washed, drained and chopped	4 oz
	125 g	low-fat ricotta cheese	4 oz
	⅛ tsp	grated nutmeg	⅛ tsp
	¼ tsp	salt	¼ tsp
		freshly ground black pepper	
	1	garlic clove, crushed	1
		rosemary sprigs for garnish (optional)	

Cut a pocket in the meaty part of each chop, through to the bone (or get the butcher to do this for you). Set aside. Put the tomatoes in a heavy-bottomed saucepan with the rosemary, adding a little water if using fresh tomatoes. Simmer for 10 minutes, stirring occasionally.

Meanwhile, heat 1 tablespoon of the oil in a large, non-stick frying pan over low heat. Add the onion and cook gently, stirring occasionally, until softened — about 5 minutes. Add the chopped spinach and cook, stirring, until it has wilted and the excess moisture has evaporated — 3 to 4 minutes.

Transfer the spinach mixture to a bowl. Add half the ricotta, the nutmeg, salt and some pepper to the spinach, mix and set aside.

Preheat the oven to 180°C (350°F or Mark 4). Mix together the remaining ricotta and the garlic; divide into four portions and use to stuff the pockets in the chops. Close the openings with wooden toothpicks.

Heat the remaining oil in a large, non-stick frying pan over medium-high heat and brown the chops on both sides — about 5 minutes in all. Transfer the chops to a baking dish in which they fit comfortably side by side *(above)*. Spread the spinach and ricotta mixture over them. Discard the rosemary sprigs, if using, from the tomatoes and spoon the tomatoes over the chops to cover the cheese mixture. Bake for 30 minutes. Remove the toothpicks and serve hot, garnished, if you like, with small rosemary sprigs.

SUGGESTED ACCOMPANIMENT: *risotto with aubergine and sweet red pepper.*

2 *Tropical fruits provide a refreshing garnish for spicy pan-fried sirloin steaks (recipe, page 69).*

Swift Sautés and Stir-Fries

Sautéing and stir-frying are techniques with a great deal in common. Both involve frying food in a pan, in a little fat, over direct heat. The only difference between the two techniques is the type of pan employed.

Traditionally, sautéing employs a heavy-based sauté pan. Nowadays, some cooks prefer to use a lighter, non-stick frying pan. But, basically, the shape of the pan is the same — that is, shallow-sided, with a wide, flat base. It is the style of vessel adopted by Western cuisines, and its name sauté is derived from the French *sauter*, meaning to jump. Professional cooks make the food literally jump with a flick of the hand grasping the sauté pan's handle: the less adventurous can prevent burning and sticking equally well by stirring and turning.

The cousin of the sauté pan employed in China and South-East Asia is the wok. With its small base and its tall curved sides, the wok permits finely sliced or shredded food to be stirred and tossed vigorously without risk of it flying off-course.

With both sautéing and stir-frying a small amount of oil or fat is used to cook the meat in the preliminary stage; during this time, a fairly high heat is used to seal in the meat's precious juices and brown the surface. The two techniques are, therefore, essentially dry-cooking methods, even though many sautés and stir-fries introduce a liquid of some kind at a later stage. Table wine, fortified wine, stock, sake, soy sauce, vinegar, tomato purée and fruit juices can all enhance beef and veal dishes. Another valuable addition is a marinade in which the food has been steeped, as with the stir-fried ginger beef with watercress on page 73.

For the health-conscious cook, the wok offers an advantage during the preliminary browning process: it minimizes the fat or oil needed. The oil collects in the compact base, so a small volume supplies a sufficient depth to cook the food. But a wok has its limitations. It is not suitable for cooking large pieces of meat, such as whole escalopes of veal. These must be browned in a sauté pan, so that the slices can be arranged in a single layer without overlapping.

The sauté pan is also indispensable for those dishes where a sauce is created by rapid reduction — thus eliminating the need for the thickenings of cream or butter and flour that appeared in so many old-fashioned beef and veal recipes. The sauté pan's wide, flat base permits a large volume of liquid to boil down quickly into an intensely flavoured sauce. In the medallions of veal with rosemary *(page 78)*, for example, stock and red wine are concentrated to make a sauce of rich flavour and velvety texture, which needs no additional thickening. The other recipes in this chapter offer equally delicious adaptations of traditions from East and West.

Stir-Fried Beef with Pine-Nuts on Chinese Cabbage

Serves 4
Working (and total) time: about 20 minutes

Calories **225**
Protein **19g**
Cholesterol **55mg**
Total fat **13g**
Saturated fat **3g**
Sodium **165mg**

500 g	beef fillet, trimmed of fat and cut into thin strips	1 lb
4 tsp	cornflour	4 tsp
1 tsp	freshly ground black pepper	1 tsp
1 tsp	oyster sauce	1 tsp
1 tsp	low-sodium soy sauce or shoyu	1 tsp
1 tbsp	dry sherry	1 tbsp
½ tsp	sugar	½ tsp
1½ tbsp	safflower oil	1½ tbsp
60 g	onion, finely chopped	2 oz
½	sweet green pepper, seeded, deribbed and finely chopped	½
1	stick celery, finely chopped	1
1	spring onion, trimmed and thinly sliced	1
8	Chinese cabbage leaves or iceberg lettuce leaves, washed and dried	8
2 tbsp	pine-nuts	2 tbsp

Put the beef strips into a bowl and sprinkle them with 2 teaspoons of the cornflour and the pepper. Toss the strips to coat them and let them stand at room temper-ature while you prepare the remaining ingredients.

In a small bowl, combine the remaining 2 teaspoons of cornflour, the oyster sauce, soy sauce, sherry and sugar. Set the bowl aside.

Heat the oil in a large, non-stick frying pan or a well-seasoned wok over high heat. When the oil is hot, add the beef strips and stir-fry them until the meat lightens in colour but is still slightly pink — 1 to 2 minutes. Use a slotted spoon to transfer the meat to a plate; set the plate aside.

Return the pan or wok to high heat. Add the onion, green pepper and celery and stir-fry them for 30 sec-onds. Return the meat to the pan, then cook the mix-ture, stirring continuously, until it is hot — 10 to 15 seconds. Pour the oyster-sauce mixture over the ingre-dients in the pan or wok. Stir-fry the meat and vege-tables until the sauce thickens and coats them — 30 seconds to 1 minute. Remove the pan from the heat.

Toss the spring onion with the beef and vegetables. Set two cabbage or lettuce leaves on each plate; divide the mixture among the leaves. Sprinkle the pine-nuts over the beef and vegetables and serve immediately.

SUGGESTED ACCOMPANIMENT: *rice noodle and shredded carrot salad.*

EDITOR'S NOTE: *If oyster sauce is not available, you can substi-tute an additional teaspoon of low-sodium soy sauce.*

Rump Steak Sautéed with Broccoli

Serves 6
Working (and total) time: about 40 minutes

Calories **250**
Protein **27g**
Cholesterol **60mg**
Total fat **11g**
Saturated fat **3g**
Sodium **355mg**

750 g	rump steak, trimmed of fat and cut into very thin strips about 4 cm (1½ inches) long	1½ lb
1½ tsp	chili paste, or ½ tsp hot red pepper flakes	1½ tsp
4	garlic cloves, very finely chopped	4
35 cl	unsalted brown stock or unsalted chicken stock (recipes, page 138)	12 fl oz
1 tbsp	cornflour	1 tbsp
500 g	broccoli, the stalks peeled and cut into thin strips about 4 cm (1½ inches) long, the tops cut into small florets	1 lb
600 g	cauliflower (about ½ large head), cut into small florets	1¼ lb
2 tbsp	safflower oil	2 tbsp
½ tsp	salt	½ tsp
2	lemons, peeled and cut into 1 cm (½ inch) pieces	2

Put the steak strips into a bowl with the chili paste or pepper flakes and the garlic, and let them marinate while you prepare the other ingredients.

Pour the stock into a small saucepan and boil it until about 15 cl (¼ pint) remains. In a small bowl, mix 2 tablespoons of the reduced stock with the cornflour.

Blanch the broccoli and cauliflower together in 3 litres (5 pints) of boiling water for 1 minute. Drain the vegetables, refresh them under cold running water, and drain them once more.

Heat 1 tablespoon of the oil in a large, non-stick frying pan or a well-seasoned wok over high heat. When the oil is hot, add the vegetables, then sprinkle them with the salt, and sauté the mixture for 2 minutes. With a slotted spoon, transfer them to a bowl.

Pour the remaining oil into the pan or wok. Add the marinated steak strips and sauté them until they are lightly browned — about 1 minute.

Return the vegetables to the pan or wok. Pour in the stock and the cornflour mixture, then add half the lemon pieces. Cook the mixture, stirring, for 1½ minutes, then use a slotted spoon to transfer it to a serving dish. Boil the sauce remaining in the pan until it is reduced to about 12.5 cl (4 fl oz), and pour it over the meat and vegetables. Scatter the remaining lemon pieces over the top and serve immediately.

Beef and
Wheat Berry Salad

Serves 6
Working time: about 25 minutes
Total time: about 45 minutes

Calories **355**
Protein **29g**
Cholesterol **65mg**
Total fat **10g**
Saturated fat **3g**
Sodium **235mg**

750 g	sirloin steak, trimmed of fat and cut into strips about 4 cm (1½ inches) long and 3 mm (⅛ inch) thick	1½ lb
285 g	wheat berries, rinsed	9½ oz
½ tsp	salt	½ tsp
2	leeks, trimmed, or 2 bunches spring onions, trimmed	2
1 tbsp	olive oil	1 tbsp
2 tsp	fresh thyme, or ¾ tsp dried thyme	2 tsp
8	large radishes, quartered	8
4 tbsp	cider vinegar	4 tbsp
1½ tbsp	fresh lemon juice	1½ tbsp
	freshly ground black pepper	

Bring 60 cl (1 pint) of water to the boil in a saucepan. Add the wheat berries and ¼ teaspoon of the salt. Reduce the heat to low and cover the pan, leaving the lid ajar. Simmer the wheat berries until they are just tender

— about 45 minutes. Drain them and set them aside.

Meanwhile, if you are using leeks, slice them into rounds about 1 cm (½ inch) wide. Wash the rounds in two or three changes of cold water to rid them of grit. Drain the rounds and set them aside. (If you are using spring onions, simply slice them.)

Ten minutes before the wheat berries are ready, heat 2 teaspoons of the oil in a large, non-stick frying pan over high heat. Add the beef and thyme, and cook them, stirring frequently, for 2 minutes; transfer the beef to a large bowl.

Return the pan to the heat and add the remaining teaspoon of oil. Add the leeks or spring onions and the radishes, and cook them, stirring frequently, for 3 minutes. Pour in the vinegar, lemon juice, the reserved beef and wheat berries, the remaining salt, and a generous grinding of black pepper. Continue cooking, stirring frequently, for 1 minute more. With a slotted spoon, transfer the mixture to a large serving bowl.

Return the pan to high heat and boil the liquid until it is reduced to 4 tablespoons. Pour the reduced liquid over the salad and toss well. Serve the salad warm or chilled.

SUGGESTED ACCOMPANIMENTS: *sliced fruit; French bread.*

Beef Fillet Stir-Fried with Butternut Squash and Turnips

Serves 4
Working time: about 15 minutes
Total time: about 25 minutes

Calories **215**
Protein **20g**
Cholesterol **55mg**
Total fat **10g**
Saturated fat **3g**
Sodium **235mg**

500 g	beef fillet, trimmed of fat and sliced into 5 cm (2 inch) long strips	1 lb
30 cl	unsalted brown stock or unsalted chicken stock (recipes, page 138)	½ pint
1	small onion, thinly sliced	1
250 g	turnips, peeled, quartered and cut into 5 mm (¼ inch) thick slices	8 oz
350 g	butternut squash, peeled, quartered and cut into 5 mm (¼ inch) thick slices	12 oz
2 tbsp	chopped fresh tarragon, or 2 tsp dried tarragon	2 tbsp
¼ tsp	salt	¼ tsp
	freshly ground black pepper	
1 tbsp	safflower oil	1 tbsp
1	garlic clove, finely chopped	1
1 tbsp	cornflour, mixed with 1 tbsp water	1 tbsp
1 tsp	distilled white vinegar	1 tsp

Place the stock and the onion in a saucepan. Set a vege-table steamer in the pan and bring the stock to a simmer. In the meantime, sprinkle the turnips and the squash separately with 1 tablespoon of the fresh tarragon or all of the dried. Put the turnips into the steamer, cover it, and steam the turnips for 2 minutes. Add the squash and continue steaming the vegetables until they are tender — about 3 minutes. Transfer the vegetables to a plate and set them aside; remove the steamer from the saucepan and reserve the stock and onion.

Season the beef with the salt and pepper. Heat ½ tablespoon of the oil in a well-seasoned wok or a heavy frying pan over high heat, and sear the beef, tossing continuously to prevent it from sticking, for about 2 minutes. Turn off the heat, transfer the meat to a plate, and keep it warm. Wipe out the wok or pan with a paper towel and set it over high heat again. Add the remaining oil, the garlic and the reserved vegetables, and cook them briefly, stirring continuously, for 3 minutes. Add the beef, toss well, and push the ingredients to the sides of the wok or pan. Pour in the reserved stock and onions and bring them to a simmer. Whisk in the cornflour mixture and the vinegar, whisking continuously until the liquid thickens — about 2 minutes. Serve the beef and vegetables with the sauce. If you are using fresh tarragon, sprinkle the remaining tablespoon over the top.

SUGGESTED ACCOMPANIMENT: *rice tossed with chives.*

Entrecôte Steak with Mushrooms and Red Onions

Serves 8
Working time: about 1 hour
Total time: about 3 hours (includes marinating)

Calories **245**
Protein **29g**
Cholesterol **70mg**
Total fat **8g**
Saturated fat **3g**
Sodium **70mg**

1.25 kg	entrecôte or rump steak in one piece, trimmed of fat	2½ lb
2	red onions, cut into 1 cm (½ inch) thick slices	2
35 cl	red wine	12 fl oz
4 tbsp	raspberry vinegar or distilled white vinegar	4 tbsp
4 tbsp	fresh lime juice	4 tbsp
20	juniper berries	20
500 g	fresh mushrooms, wiped clean	1 lb
17.5 cl	unsalted brown stock or unsalted chicken stock (recipes, page 138)	6 fl oz
2 tbsp	cornflour	2 tbsp
	freshly ground black pepper	
4 tbsp	finely chopped parsley	4 tbsp

Spread the onion slices in the bottom of a shallow baking dish. Set the steak on the onions; pour the wine, vinegar and lime juice over the steak, then scatter the juniper berries over all. Let the steak marinate at room temperature for 2 hours or put it into the refrigerator overnight.

Remove the steak and onions from the marinade, and pat them dry with paper towels. Strain the marinade into a bowl and set it aside. Discard the berries.

Heat a large, non-stick frying pan over high heat. Add the onion slices and sauté them until they are tender — about 4 minutes each side. Remove them from the pan and keep them warm. Cook the steak in the pan over medium-high heat for 4 minutes on each side for medium-rare meat. Remove the steak from the pan and let it rest while you prepare the mushrooms.

Sauté the mushrooms in the pan over high heat, stirring occasionally, until most of the juices have evaporated — about 5 minutes. Remove them with a slotted spoon and set them aside. Pour the steak marinade into the pan and boil it until it has reduced by half — about 10 minutes. Mix the stock and the cornflour together and whisk them into the reduced marinade. Bring the liquid to the boil and continue cooking until it thickens slightly — about 1 minute. Season the mushrooms with some black pepper and stir them, along with the parsley, into the sauce.

Slice the steak and arrange it on a serving platter with the onions. Spoon the mushrooms round the steak just before serving.

SUGGESTED ACCOMPANIMENT: *French bread.*

Beef Stroganoff with Wild Mushrooms

Serves 4
Working time: about 40 minutes
Total time: about 1 hour

Calories **220**
Protein **24g**
Cholesterol **50mg**
Total fat **12g**
Saturated fat **3g**
Sodium **150mg**

350 g	beef fillet, trimmed of fat	12 oz
15 g	dried ceps (porcini), or other wild mushrooms, soaked in 15 cl (¼ pint) warm water for 20 minutes	½ oz
2 tbsp	virgin olive oil	2 tbsp
125 g	shallots, thinly sliced	4 oz
125 g	button mushrooms, wiped clean and sliced	4 oz
½ tsp	dried green peppercorns, crushed	½ tsp
¼ tsp	salt	¼ tsp
5 tbsp	Greek-style strained yogurt	5 tbsp
½ tsp	Dijon mustard	½ tsp
2	firm ripe tomatoes, skinned, seeded and cut into thin strips	2
1	small gherkin, cut into short thin strips	1

Cut the beef fillets crosswise (against the grain) into slices about 5 mm (¼ inch) thick. Cut the slices into strips about 4 cm (1½ inches) long. Drain the soaked mushrooms, reserving the soaking water, and remove any remaining sand or grit under running water; then chop them coarsely. Strain the soaking water through a sieve lined with paper towels.

Heat 2 teaspoons of the oil in a large, non-stick frying pan over medium heat. Add the shallots and cook for 2 minutes, stirring, then add the wild mushrooms, soaking water and button mushrooms. Cook, stirring frequently, until the excess liquid has evaporated — about 10 minutes. Remove the mushroom mixture from the pan. Heat another 2 teaspoons of the oil in the pan over high heat and add half the beef. Fry briskly for 3 to 4 minutes, stirring and tossing to brown the strips evenly. Add the browned strips to the mushroom mixture. Heat the remaining oil in the pan and brown the remaining beef strips in the same way. Return the first batch of beef and the mushroom mixture to the pan and stir. Mix in the peppercorns and salt.

In a small bowl, stir together the yogurt and mustard. Add to the pan with the tomato strips and gherkin strips. Fold together gently but thoroughly, and heat without boiling. Serve hot.

SUGGESTED ACCOMPANIMENTS: *noodles; curly endive salad.*

Steaks Creole

Serves 4
Working time: about 45 minutes
Total time: about 5 hours (includes marinating)

Calories **320**
Protein **29g**
Cholesterol **60mg**
Total fat **11g**
Saturated fat **3g**
Sodium **120mg**

500 g	sirloin or entrecôte steaks, trimmed of fat, cut into four 2 cm (¾ inch) thick pieces	1 lb
350 g	fresh pineapple, peeled, skinned and sliced crosswise	12 oz
350 g	watermelon, peeled and sliced	12 oz
1	papaya, peeled, halved, seeded and sliced	1
1	mango, peeled, stoned and sliced	1
1 tbsp	virgin olive oil	1 tbsp
2 tbsp	lime juice	2 tbsp
2 tsp	chopped fresh mint	2 tsp
⅛ tsp	salt	⅛ tsp
Rum marinade		
2 tbsp	dark rum	2 tbsp
½ tbsp	virgin olive oil	½ tbsp
2	garlic cloves, crushed	2
12	whole allspice berries, crushed	12
1 tsp	cayenne pepper	1 tsp
	freshly ground black pepper	

To make the marinade, mix together the rum, oil, garlic, allspice, cayenne pepper and some black pepper. Put the beef in a shallow dish and brush the marinade over both sides of each steak. Cover loosely and leave to marinate in a cold place or the refrigerator for at least 4 hours, preferably overnight.

Before cooking, let the steaks stand at room temperature for 30 minutes. Meanwhile, arrange the sliced fruit on individual plates. Whisk together the oil, lime juice, mint and salt, and set aside.

Place the steaks in a heavy, non-stick frying pan over high heat. Cook for 4 minutes on each side for rare steaks, longer if you prefer them well done. Arrange the steaks on the plates with the fruit. Dribble the dressing over the fruit or serve it separately. Serve at once.

EDITOR'S NOTE: *This dish is best served without additional accompaniments, which would mar the complementary flavours of the meat and fruit.*

South-East Asian Beef Noodles

Serves 4
Working (and total) time: about 45 minutes

Calories **420**
Protein **33g**
Cholesterol **70mg**
Total fat **13g**
Saturated fat **3g**
Sodium **260mg**

600 g	rump steak, trimmed of fat and cut into paper-thin slices	1¼ lb
1 tbsp	low-sodium soy sauce or shoyu	1 tbsp
2 tbsp	dry sherry or dry white wine	2 tbsp
2 tbsp	sugar	2 tbsp
	freshly ground black pepper	
1½ tbsp	cornflour	1½ tbsp
175 g	Asian wheat noodles, or 125 g (4 oz) vermicelli	6 oz

4 tsp	safflower oil	4 tsp
1	small onion, halved and sliced lengthwise	1
1	carrot, peeled, halved lengthwise and thinly sliced on the diagonal	1
250 g	broccoli stems, peeled, halved lengthwise and thinly sliced on the diagonal	8 oz
½	sweet red pepper, seeded, deribbed and cut into narrow strips about 5 cm (2 inches) long	½
2 tsp	finely chopped fresh ginger root	2 tsp
4	garlic cloves, finely chopped	4
¼ litre	unsalted brown or chicken stock (recipes, page 138)	8 fl oz
½ tbsp	sweet chili sauce, or ½ tsp hot red pepper flakes mixed with ½ tsp golden syrup and ½ tsp rice vinegar	½ tbsp
1 tbsp	fresh lemon juice	1 tbsp
1 tbsp	hoisin sauce or low-sodium soy sauce	1 tbsp

In a large bowl, combine the beef slices with the tablespoon of soy sauce, the sherry or white wine, 1 tablespoon of the sugar, some pepper and ½ tablespoon of the cornflour. Set the mixture aside.

Put the noodles into 3 litres (5 pints) of boiling water. Start testing the noodles or vermicelli after 3 to 5 minutes and cook them until they are *al dente*. Drain the pasta in a colander and rinse it under very hot water. Drain the pasta again and transfer it to a serving platter. Cover the platter with foil to keep the pasta warm.

Heat 2 teaspoons of the oil in a large, non-stick frying pan or well-seasoned wok over high heat. Add the onion slices and stir-fry them for 1 minute. Add the carrot and broccoli, and stir-fry them for 1 minute. Mix in the sweet red pepper and stir-fry the mixture for 2 minutes more. Mound the vegetables on top of the pasta, then cover the platter with the foil once more, and keep it warm.

Heat the remaining 2 teaspoons of oil in the pan or wok over high heat. Add the ginger and garlic, and stir-fry them until the ginger is light brown — about 2 minutes. Add the beef along with its marinade, and stir-fry it until no traces of pink remain — 1 to 2 minutes. Spoon the beef mixture on to the centre of the vegetables and keep the platter warm.

Pour the stock into the pan or wok, and bring it to the boil. While the stock is heating, mix the remaining cornflour with 2 tablespoons of water in a small bowl. Stir into the stock the cornflour mixture, chili sauce or red-pepper-flake mixture, the remaining sugar, the lemon juice, and the hoisin sauce or soy sauce. Reduce the heat and simmer the mixture until it thickens — about 1 minute. Pour the sauce over the beef and serve it immediately.

Orange-Fried Beef

Serves 6
Working (and total) time: about 45 minutes

Calories **270**
Protein **24g**
Cholesterol **65mg**
Total fat **10g**
Saturated fat **3g**
Sodium **140mg**

750 g	sirloin steak, trimmed of fat and sliced into very thin strips	1 ½ lb
2	oranges	2
1 tbsp	grated lemon rind	1 tbsp
3 tbsp	cornflour	3 tbsp
2 tbsp	sugar	2 tbsp
2 tbsp	safflower oil	2 tbsp
2 tsp	julienned fresh ginger root	2 tsp
¼ tsp	salt	¼ tsp
⅛ tsp	cayenne pepper	⅛ tsp
4 tbsp	rice vinegar or distilled white vinegar	4 tbsp
500 g	mange-tout, stems and strings removed	1 lb

Carefully pare the rind from the oranges with a sharp knife, leaving the white pith behind. Slice the rind into fine julienne and reserve it.

Squeeze the juice from the oranges and pour it into a small saucepan. Boil the juice over medium heat until only 3 tablespoons remain and set it aside.

Put the beef into a large bowl and sprinkle it with the lemon rind, cornflour and sugar. Mix well to coat the beef and set the beef aside.

Heat 1 tablespoon of the safflower oil in a large, non-stick frying pan or a well-seasoned wok over high heat. Add the orange rind and the ginger to the pan or wok, and cook them, stirring constantly, for 1 minute. Remove the rind and ginger with a slotted spoon, and set the mixture aside.

Add one third of the beef to the hot pan or wok, distributing it in a single layer. Brown the beef well — it should take 3 to 4 minutes to cook — stirring it frequently. With a slotted spoon, remove the cooked beef. Add ½ tablespoon of the oil to the pan or wok and repeat the process with another third of the beef. Remove the second batch. Heat the remaining ½ tablespoon of oil and cook the rest of the meat.

Once the third batch is well browned, return the already-cooked beef and the rind-and-ginger mixture to the pan or wok. Sprinkle the meat with the salt and the cayenne pepper, then pour in the vinegar and the reduced orange juice. Cook the meat rapidly, stirring often, until all of the liquid has evaporated — approximately 2 minutes.

While the beef is cooking, pour enough water into a saucepan to cover the bottom by 2.5 cm (1 inch). Set a vegetable steamer in the water, bring the water to the boil, and add the mange-tout. Cover the pan tightly and steam for 2 minutes.

Transfer the mange-tout to a warmed serving platter and mound the beef on top. Serve immediately.

SUGGESTED ACCOMPANIMENT: *steamed rice.*

Sautéed Beef Tossed with Red Cabbage and Apples

Serves 8
Working time: about 30 minutes
Total time: about 45 minutes

Calories **220**
Protein **19g**
Cholesterol **50mg**
Total fat **7g**
Saturated fat **2g**
Sodium **145mg**

850 g	sirloin steak, trimmed of fat and cut into thin strips about 4 cm (1½ inches) long	1¾ lb
45 g	shallots, chopped	1½ oz
¼ tsp	salt	¼ tsp
¼ litre	unsalted brown stock or unsalted chicken stock (recipes, page 138)	8 fl oz
½ litre	red wine	16 fl oz
2 tsp	caraway seeds	2 tsp
1.25 kg	red cabbage, cored, quartered and sliced	2½ lb
2	tart green apples, cored, quartered and cut into strips 5 cm (2 inches) long and 5 mm (¼ inch) wide	2
1 tbsp	honey	1 tbsp
4 tbsp	fresh lemon juice	4 tbsp
1 tsp	freshly ground black pepper	1 tsp
1½ tbsp	safflower oil	1½ tbsp
2	spring onions, trimmed and sliced	2

Combine the shallots, salt, stock, wine and 1 teaspoon of the caraway seeds in a non-reactive saucepan over medium heat. Simmer the liquid until it is reduced to 12.5 cl (4 fl oz) — about 40 minutes.

Meanwhile, place the cabbage in a large bowl with the apples and the remaining caraway seeds. Mix the honey and lemon juice, and pour it over the cabbage mixture. Toss the mixture well and set it aside.

Place the meat in a bowl and sprinkle it with the pepper. Pour the reduced liquid over the meat and stir the mixture well.

Heat 1 tablespoon of the oil in a large sauté pan or heavy frying pan set over high heat. Add the beef and spring onions and sauté them, stirring, until the meat is browned — about 1½ minutes. Transfer the mixture to a bowl.

Heat the remaining oil in the pan over medium-high heat. Add the cabbage-and-apple mixture and cook it, stirring frequently, until the cabbage has wilted slightly — 3 to 4 minutes. Return the beef to the pan, toss the mixture well, and serve it at once.

SUGGESTED ACCOMPANIMENT: *broad egg noodles.*

Stir-Fried Ginger Beef with Watercress

Serves 4
Working time: about 20 minutes
Total time: about 1 hour and 10 minutes

Calories **195**
Protein **21g**
Cholesterol **55mg**
Total fat **7g**
Saturated fat **2g**
Sodium **440mg**

500 g	rump steak, trimmed of fat and sliced into thin strips 7.5 cm (3 inches) long	1 lb
½ tbsp	groundnut oil	½ tbsp
1	bunch watercress, trimmed, washed and dried	1
Ginger marinade		
5 cm	piece fresh ginger root, peeled and finely chopped	2 inch
1 tbsp	chili paste, or 1 tsp hot red pepper flakes	1 tbsp
4 tbsp	dry sherry	4 tbsp
4 tbsp	unsalted chicken stock (recipe, page 138)	4 tbsp
1 tsp	cornflour	1 tsp
1 tsp	sugar	1 tsp
Cucumber salad		
500 g	cucumbers, seeded and cut into thick strips	1 lb
¼ tsp	salt	¼ tsp
4 tbsp	rice vinegar or distilled white vinegar	4 tbsp
1 tsp	dark sesame oil	1 tsp

Combine all of the marinade ingredients in a bowl. Add the beef and toss it well; cover the bowl and marinate the meat for 1 hour at room temperature.

Combine the cucumbers, salt, vinegar and sesame oil in a bowl. Refrigerate the salad.

When the marinating time is up, drain the beef, reserving the marinade. Heat the oil in a large, non-stick frying pan or a well-seasoned wok over high heat. Add the beef and stir-fry it until it is well browned — about 2 minutes. Add the reserved marinade; stir constantly until the sauce thickens — about 1 minute. Add the watercress and toss the mixture quickly. Serve the stir-fried beef and watercress immediately, accompanied by the chilled cucumber salad.

SUGGESTED ACCOMPANIMENT: *rice with sweet red peppers.*

Oaty Veal Escalopes Viennese-Style

Serves 4
Working (and total) time: about 45 minutes

Calories **255**
Protein **22g**
Cholesterol **90mg**
Total fat **12g**
Saturated fat **2g**
Sodium **210mg**

4	veal escalopes (about 90 g/3 oz each), trimmed of fat and flattened (page 32, Step 1)	4
30 g	flour	1 oz
¼ tsp	salt	¼ tsp
	freshly ground black pepper	
1	egg white	1
60 g	fine oatmeal	2 oz
2 tbsp	safflower oil	2 tbsp
	lemon wedges for garnish	

Put the flour, salt and pepper on a large plate or sheet of greaseproof paper, mix together and spread out evenly. Lightly beat the egg white with 1 tablespoon of water in a small bowl. Spread out the oatmeal on another plate or sheet of greaseproof paper.

Dip one escalope in the seasoned flour to coat both sides, and shake off excess flour. Place the escalope on a flat surface and lightly brush and dab the egg white over one side. Turn the escalope over, and place on the plate of oatmeal, egg side down. Press down gently. Brush and dab the top side of the escalope with egg white, turn it over and press gently into the oatmeal. Cover any still exposed areas of escalope with oatmeal so that it is evenly coated, pressing it on gently with your fingertips. Shake off excess oatmeal. Coat the remaining escalopes in the same way.

Heat 1 tablespoon of the oil in a large, heavy non-stick frying pan over medium heat. Add two of the escalopes and cook for 7 to 10 minutes in all, turning to brown evenly. When cooked, transfer the escalopes to a warm platter and cook the remaining escalopes in the same way. Garnish with the lemon wedges and serve.

SUGGESTED ACCOMPANIMENT: *spinach.*

Veal, Prosciutto and Sage Sauté

Serves 4
Working (and total) time: about 15 minutes

Calories **175**
Protein **23g**
Cholesterol **95mg**
Total fat **7g**
Saturated fat **2g**
Sodium **350mg**

400 g	veal escalope, trimmed of fat, cut into strips 5 mm (¼ inch) wide and 4 cm (1½ inches) long	14 oz
1 tbsp	virgin olive oil	1 tbsp
45 g	thinly sliced prosciutto, trimmed of excess fat, cut into strips 5 mm (¼ inch) wide and 4 cm (1½ inches) long	1½ oz
¼ tsp	salt	¼ tsp
	freshly ground black pepper	
3 tbsp	coarsely chopped fresh sage, or 2 tsp dried sage	3 tbsp
4 tbsp	Marsala	4 tbsp

Heat the oil in a large, non-stick frying pan over high heat. Add the strips of veal and sauté for about 1½ minutes, stirring to cook and brown the veal evenly. If the veal exudes a lot of liquid, cook until this has evaporated.

Add the prosciutto, salt and some pepper and cook the meat, stirring and tossing, for 1 minute. Add the sage and Marsala, toss for a further 30 seconds and serve immediately.

SUGGESTED ACCOMPANIMENTS: *creamed potato and celeriac; watercress and orange salad.*

Veal Scaloppini with Lemon and Asparagus

Serves 4
Working (and total) time: about 30 minutes

Calories **180**
Protein **23g**
Cholesterol **90mg**
Total fat **10g**
Saturated fat **3g**
Sodium **380mg**

4	veal escalopes (about 90 g/3 oz each) trimmed of fat and flattened (page 32, Step 1)	4
4	large asparagus spears	4
1 tbsp	virgin olive oil	1 tbsp
1	garlic clove, quartered	1
½	lemon, juice only	½
½ tbsp	chopped fresh rosemary, or ½ tsp dried rosemary, crumbled	½ tbsp
¼ tsp	salt	¼ tsp
	freshly ground black pepper	
1½ tbsp	freshly grated Parmesan cheese	1½ tbsp

Cook the asparagus in a small, shallow pan of boiling water for 3 to 4 minutes, or until just tender but still firm. Drain the asparagus and refresh them under cold running water to prevent further cooking. Drain again, cut the asparagus spears in half lengthwise and set them aside while you cook the meat.

Cut each escalope crosswise into three pieces. Heat the oil with the garlic in a large, non-stick frying pan over high heat. Add half the veal and cook for about 1½ minutes until golden-brown on both sides. Transfer the veal to a gratin dish, and cook the remaining veal in the same way. Arrange the pieces of veal in the bottom of the dish, slightly overlapping. Sprinkle them with the lemon juice, rosemary, salt and some pepper. Discard the garlic.

Preheat the grill. Arrange the halved asparagus spears neatly in a row down the centre of the veal pieces. Sprinkle the Parmesan cheese over the veal and asparagus. Grill for 3 to 5 minutes or until the veal and asparagus are piping hot and the topping is golden-brown. Serve immediately.

SUGGESTED ACCOMPANIMENT: *mushroom risotto.*

Sichuan Stir-Fried Veal and Crunchy Vegetables

Serves 4
Working time: about 40 minutes
Total time: about 2 hours and 40 minutes
(includes marinating)

Calories **300**
Protein **30g**
Cholesterol **110mg**
Total fat **14g**
Saturated fat **3g**
Sodium **215mg**

500 g	veal escalopes, trimmed of fat, flattened (page 32, Step 1) and cut diagonally into strips 4 cm (1½ inches) long by 5 mm (¼ inch) wide	1 lb
4 tbsp	low-sodium soy sauce or shoyu	4 tbsp
4 tbsp	sake or dry sherry	4 tbsp
2	dried red chili peppers, finely chopped (caution, page 8)	2
2 tbsp	safflower oil	2 tbsp
6	spring onions, sliced diagonally	6
2.5 cm	fresh ginger root, cut into very fine julienne	1 inch
1 to 2	garlic cloves, crushed	1 to 2
125 g	whole baby sweetcorns	4 oz
250 g	carrots, julienned	8 oz
125 g	cauliflower florets	4 oz
125 g	French beans, topped and tailed	4 oz
30 cl	unsalted chicken or veal stock (recipes, page 138)	½ pint
1 tbsp	tomato paste	1 tbsp
1½ tbsp	cornflour, mixed with 1 tbsp cold water	1½ tbsp
	freshly ground black pepper	
1 tbsp	sesame oil	1 tbsp

In a bowl, combine the strips of veal, 2 tablespoons each of the soy sauce and sake, and the chilies. Cover and leave to marinate for 2 hours, turning occasionally.

Heat a wok or a large, deep, heavy frying pan over medium-high heat and pour in the safflower oil. Add the spring onions, ginger and garlic, and stir-fry for 30 seconds to flavour the oil. Add the veal and its marinade and stir-fry, tossing frequently, until all the strips have changed colour — about 3 minutes. Remove the veal and flavourings with a slotted spoon and set aside on a plate; do not discard the oil.

Add the baby sweetcorn to the pan and stir-fry, tossing constantly, for 2 minutes, then add the carrots, cauliflower and beans, and stir-fry for a further 2 minutes. Return the veal and flavourings to the pan and stir-fry to combine with the vegetables. Push the contents to the sides and pour the stock into the centre. Stir in the tomato paste, remaining soy sauce and sake, the cornflour mixture and some pepper. Bring to the boil and boil until the liquid thickens — 1 to 2 minutes. Redistribute the veal and vegetables in the sauce and stir to coat all the pieces evenly.

Serve the veal and vegetables with the sesame oil sprinkled over the top.

SUGGESTED ACCOMPANIMENT: *Chinese egg noodles.*

Medallions of Veal with Rosemary and Red Wine

Serves 6
Working time: about 15 minutes
Total time: about 1 hour and 15 minutes (includes marinating)

Calories **200**
Protein **21g**
Cholesterol **95mg**
Total fat **12g**
Saturated fat **3g**
Sodium **215mg**

6	medallions of veal (about 125 g/4 oz each), trimmed of fat	6
	fresh rosemary sprigs	
2 tbsp	virgin olive oil	2 tbsp

1	garlic clove, crushed	1
1	lemon, finely grated rind only	1
1 tbsp	chopped parsley	1 tbsp
15 g	unsalted butter	½ oz
¼ litre	red wine	8 fl oz
15 cl	unsalted veal or chicken stock (recipes, page 138)	¼ pint
¼ tsp	salt	¼ tsp
	freshly ground black pepper	

Spear each medallion of veal with two or three small sprigs of rosemary. Blend 1½ tablespoons of the oil with the garlic, lemon rind and parsley in a shallow dish. Add the medallions to this marinade and turn them carefully until they are well coated. Cover and marinate at room temperature for at least 1 hour.

Heat the remaining oil with the butter in a non-stick sauté or frying pan. Add the medallions and cook for 2 to 3 minutes on each side until well browned but still slightly pink inside. Transfer the veal to a plate lined with absorbent paper towels. Cover and keep hot.

Pour off all the excess fat from the sauté pan, and stir in the wine and stock. Bring to the boil, stirring, then boil gently until the liquid is reduced by half. Season with the salt and some pepper.

Arrange the medallions on a hot serving plate, strain the sauce over them and, if liked, garnish with more rosemary sprigs. Serve immediately.

SUGGESTED ACCOMPANIMENTS: *French beans; asparagus.*

Veal Fillets with Gorgonzola and Fennel

Serves 4
Working (and total) time: about 40 minutes

Calories **240**
Protein **27g**
Cholesterol **105mg**
Total fat **12g**
Saturated fat **2g**
Sodium **380mg**

500 g	veal fillet, trimmed of fat, cut diagonally into 5 mm (¼ inch) thick slices and slightly flattened (page 32, Step 1)	1 lb
1 tbsp	virgin olive oil	1 tbsp
2 tbsp	Pernod or unsalted stock	2 tbsp
250 g	bulb fennel, cut into slices, feathery tops reserved	8 oz
90 g	Gorgonzola cheese, mashed	3 oz
2 tbsp	skimmed milk	2 tbsp
2 tsp	chopped fresh sage, or ½ tsp dried sage	2 tsp
2 tsp	chopped fresh thyme, or ½ tsp dried thyme	2 tsp
⅛ tsp	salt	⅛ tsp
	freshly ground black pepper	

Preheat the oven to 140°C (275°F or Mark 1). Heat the oil in a non-stick frying pan over medium-high heat, add as many pieces of veal as the pan will comfortably hold and cook for 3 to 5 minutes until just tender, turning once and pressing the pieces of veal firmly with a palette knife or spatula to keep them as flat as possible. Transfer the veal to a platter, cover and keep hot in the oven. Cook the remainder of the veal in the same way.

Add the Pernod or stock to the cooking juices in the pan, increase the heat and stir briskly to deglaze. Add the fennel and toss over high heat for 2 to 3 minutes, then remove with a slotted spoon and keep hot with the veal.

Reduce the heat, add the Gorgonzola and milk, and cook gently, stirring, until the cheese has melted and formed a sauce with the cooking juices and milk. Add the chopped sage, thyme, salt and some pepper, and remove the pan from the heat.

To assemble the dish, arrange the meat and fennel on individual plates. Spoon the sauce over the meat and garnish with the reserved fennel tops. Serve immediately.

EDITOR'S NOTE: *Adding Pernod to the cooking juices heightens the anise flavour of the fennel.*

3 *Flattened veal escalopes await a fruit stuffing and a gentle simmering in red grape juice (recipe, page 100).*

Moist and Gentle Cooking

Braising, poaching and stewing are all moist methods of cooking that involve simmering meat in the liquid and vapour of an enclosed vessel. They differ from each other only in that braising employs relatively little liquid compared to poaching; and, often, the meat to be braised is browned initially to produce rich residues that contribute flavour to the finished dish. Stewing generally implies the braising of meat that is cut into small pieces.

The appeal of moist methods lies in a culinary alchemy whereby the flavour of the meat, and any supporting vegetables and herbs, is drawn into the surrounding liquid. The most commonly used liquids are stock, wine and water. But there are no hard and fast rules. Beer, for example, might be employed *(page 84)*, and tomatoes, puréed to a pulp, feature often — as in the recipes on pages 87, 90, 97 and 101.

Traditionally, cooks have employed the moist methods for the tougher cuts of beef and veal, since these cuts have most to gain from the tenderizing process of prolonged moist cooking. But the health-conscious cook must question some of the old ways, since many firm cuts are excessively fatty. In breast of veal and beef flank, for example, the layers of muscle are interlarded with fat, and the marrow in the centre of a slice of veal shin is very high in fat. In place of such cuts, the recipes here make much use of beef and veal topside and beef sirloin.

These less fatty cuts, being also less gelatinous, do not necessarily need — or profit from — extensive simmering. In the case of fruit-stuffed veal olives *(page 100)*, escalopes are simmered for just 20 minutes in red grape juice, after a brief preliminary browning. In Japanese simmered beef *(page 99)* slices of beef fillet are cooked at table in broth for a mere 5 minutes.

As well as avoiding fatty cuts, this chapter also looks to supporting ingredients to play a part in keeping the calorie count low. Gone is the excess of flour, egg yolks and cream that once played a part in the thickening of cooking liquids. Many of the new sauces are thickened by reduction. In the case of the blanquette of veal *(page 104)*, the conventional thickening of several egg yolks and double cream is replaced with a single egg yolk, semi-skimmed milk and cornflour. Accompanied by mushrooms and onions and seasoned with lemon juice, the result is a light and refreshing re-interpretation of the culinary classic.

Sauerbraten

IN THIS VERSION OF A POPULAR GERMAN DISH, LEAN TOPSIDE IS
MARINATED IN RED WINE VINEGAR, SUGAR AND SPICES FOR 3 DAYS
TO PRODUCE A MOIST AND TENDER JOINT.

Serves 6
Working time: about 45 minutes
Total time: about 3 days (includes marinating)

Calories **340**
Protein **40g**
Cholesterol **75mg**
Total fat **6g**
Saturated fat **3g**
Sodium **200mg**

1 kg	topside of beef, rolled and tied, trimmed of fat	2 lb
10	whole cloves	10
¼ litre	red wine	8 fl oz
12.5 cl	red wine vinegar	4 fl oz
1	onion, grated	1
2 tsp	soft brown sugar	2 tsp
1 tsp	dry mustard	1 tsp
6	black peppercorns	6
2	bay leaves	2
½ tsp	ground allspice	½ tsp
1 tbsp	virgin olive oil	1 tbsp
30 cl	brown stock (recipe, page 138)	½ pint
1.5 kg	mixed root vegetables (turnip, parsnip, swede, carrot, potato), peeled and left whole or cut into large chunks	3 lb
3 tbsp	raisins	3 tbsp
2 tsp	arrowroot	2 tsp
	freshly ground black pepper	
⅛ tsp	salt	⅛ tsp
2 tbsp	finely chopped parsley	2 tbsp

Stud the beef with the cloves and place in an earthenware or glass (not metal) dish. In a saucepan, heat the red wine, wine vinegar, onion, sugar, mustard, peppercorns, bay leaves and allspice. Pour over the beef and leave to cool. When the beef is cold, cover the dish and marinate in the refrigerator for 3 days, turning the meat occasionally.

Thirty minutes before cooking, remove the beef from the marinade, pat it dry with paper towels and let it stand at room temperature. Reserve the marinade. Preheat the oven to 150°C (300°F or Mark 2).

Heat the oil in a fireproof casserole over high heat, add the beef and brown it on all sides, turning it constantly — about 5 minutes. Strain the reserved marinade over the beef, pour in the stock and bring to the boil. Cover and cook in the oven for 1¼ hours, turning and basting frequently to ensure even cooking. Meanwhile, put the root vegetables in a large saucepan, cover with cold water and bring to the boil. Drain immediately and set aside.

Remove the casserole from the oven and arrange the vegetables round the meat as illustrated on the left. Cover again and return to the oven for a further hour, or until the beef and vegetables are tender.

Transfer the beef to a warmed serving dish. Remove the vegetables from the cooking liquid with a slotted spoon and arrange them round the beef. Set the dish aside and keep hot. Transfer the casserole to the top of the stove and add the raisins. Mix the arrowroot to a smooth paste with 1 tablespoon of cold water and stir into the cooking liquid. Bring the liquid to the boil, stirring, then simmer until thickened — 2 to 3 minutes. Add some pepper and the salt. Serve the meat sliced, with a little of the gravy poured over. Sprinkle the vegetables with the parsley and pass the remaining gravy separately.

SUGGESTED ACCOMPANIMENT: *mashed potatoes.*

Beef Braised in Beer

Serves 8
Working time: about 30 minutes
Total time: about 3 hours

Calories **290**
Protein **31g**
Cholesterol **85mg**
Total fat **8g**
Saturated fat **3g**
Sodium **240mg**

1.25 kg	topside of beef, trimmed of fat	2½ lb
½ tsp	safflower oil	½ tsp
2 kg	large onions, sliced	4 lb
½ litre	unsalted brown or chicken stock (recipes, page 138)	16 fl oz
2 tbsp	plain flour	2 tbsp
35 cl	stout	12 fl oz
4	garlic cloves, chopped	4
2 tbsp	julienned fresh ginger root	2 tbsp
1	bay leaf	1
4	fresh thyme sprigs, or 1 tsp dried thyme	4
1	strip lemon rind	1
2 tbsp	dark molasses	2 tbsp
½ tsp	salt	½ tsp
	freshly ground black pepper	

Preheat the oven to 170°C (325°F or Mark 3). Heat the oil in a large, non-stick frying pan over high heat. Add the joint and sear it until it is well browned on all sides — about 5 minutes in all. Transfer the roast to an ovenproof casserole.

Reduce the heat under the pan to medium. Add the onions to the pan and cook them, stirring frequently, until they begin to soften — about 10 minutes. Deglaze the pan with 2 tablespoons of the stock. Continue cooking the onions, adding another 2 tablespoons of stock whenever the liquid in the pan has evaporated, until the onions are very soft and their juices have caramelized — 15 to 20 minutes more. Sprinkle the flour over the onions; cook the mixture, stirring constantly, for 1 minute.

Pour ¼ litre (8 fl oz) of the remaining stock into the pan and stir well to incorporate the flour. Increase the heat to medium high and boil the mixture until it is quite thick — 3 to 4 minutes. Pour in the rest of the stock and the stout. Bring the liquid to a simmer, then transfer the contents of the pan to the casserole. Add the garlic, ginger, bay leaf, thyme, lemon rind, molasses, salt and some pepper to the casserole. Cover and braise the joint in the oven until it is very tender — about 2 hours.

Transfer the beef to a carving board, slice it, and arrange the slices on a serving platter. Remove the bay leaf, the thyme sprigs if you used them, and the lemon rind from the sauce, and pour it over the meat.

SUGGESTED ACCOMPANIMENTS: *noodles tossed with parsley; steamed parsnips.*

Lemon-Cardamom Braised Beef

Serves 8
Working time: about 1 hour
Total time: about 3 hours

Calories **240**
Protein **29g**
Cholesterol **80mg**
Total fat **8g**
Saturated fat **3g**
Sodium **290mg**

1.5 kg	topside of beef or top rump, trimmed of fat	3 lb
2 tsp	safflower oil	2 tsp
2	onions, cut into eighths	2
2	sticks celery, coarsely chopped	2
2	garlic cloves, chopped	2
¾ litre	unsalted brown or chicken stock (recipes, page 138)	1¼ pints
12.5 cl	dry white wine	4 fl oz
1	lemon, rind only, cut into strips	1
½ tsp	ground cardamom or ground ginger	½ tsp
½ tsp	salt	½ tsp
2½ tbsp	fresh lemon juice	2½ tbsp
1 tbsp	Dijon mustard	1 tbsp
	freshly ground black pepper	
500 g	carrots	1 lb
500 g	courgettes, halved lengthwise, the halves sliced on the diagonal into 1 cm (½ inch) wide pieces	1 lb

Heat the oil in a shallow fireproof casserole or a large, deep sauté pan over high heat. Sear the beef until it is browned on all sides — 10 to 15 minutes. Tuck the onions, celery and garlic round the beef, and add the stock, wine, lemon rind, ¼ teaspoon of the cardamom or ginger, and ¼ teaspoon of the salt. Bring the liquid to the boil, then lower the heat to maintain a slow simmer. Cover the pan, leaving the lid slightly ajar, and braise the beef for 1 hour. Turn the beef over and continue cooking it until it is tender — 1½ to 2 hours. Transfer the beef to a carving board and cover it loosely with aluminium foil.

Strain the cooking liquid through a fine sieve into a saucepan. Whisk in 1½ tablespoons of the lemon juice, the mustard, a generous grinding of pepper, the remaining cardamom or ginger, and the remaining salt. Simmer the sauce over medium heat until it is reduced to 30 cl (½ pint).

While the sauce is reducing, peel the carrots and cut them with a roll cut. Using a chef's knife, slice off the tip of a carrot on the diagonal. Roll the carrot a half turn and slice off another piece — it will have non-parallel ends. Continue rolling and slicing until you reach the stem end. Repeat the procedure to prepare the remaining carrots.

Pour enough water into a saucepan to fill it 2.5 cm ▶

(1 inch) deep. Set a vegetable steamer in the pan and bring the water to the boil. Add the carrots and cover the pan tightly. Steam the carrots until they begin to soften —5 to 7 minutes. Transfer them to a large frying pan over medium-high heat. Add the courgettes, the remaining lemon juice, 12.5 cl (4 fl oz) of the sauce and a liberal grinding of pepper. Cook the vegetables, stirring frequently, until almost all of the liquid has evaporated and the vegetables are glazed — 7 to 10 minutes.

Cut the beef into thin slices and arrange them on a warmed serving platter along with the vegetables. Briefly reheat the remaining sauce and pour it over the beef. Serve immediately.

SUGGESTED ACCOMPANIMENT: *granary bread or rolls.*

Beef Braised with Fennel

Serves 4
Working time: about 15 minutes
Total time: about 1 hour and 15 minutes

Calories **245**
Protein **27g**
Cholesterol **75mg**
Total fat **10g**
Saturated fat **3g**
Sodium **250mg**

600 g	sirloin steak, trimmed of fat and cut into four pieces	1¼ lb
¼ tsp	salt	¼ tsp
	freshly ground black pepper	
1 tbsp	safflower oil	1 tbsp
1	large fennel bulb, thinly sliced	1
¼ litre	unsalted brown or chicken stock (recipes, page 138)	8 fl oz
4 tbsp	dry white wine	4 tbsp
1	large carrot, peeled and grated	1
1 tbsp	cornflour, mixed with 2 tablespoons of water	1 tbsp

With a meat bat or the flat of a heavy knife, pound the steak pieces to a thickness of 1 cm (½ inch). Season the meat with the salt and some pepper. Heat 1 teaspoon of the oil in a large, non-stick frying pan over medium-high heat and sear the meat on both sides. Transfer the meat to a plate and set it aside.

Heat the remaining oil in the pan and add the fennel. Cook the fennel, stirring occasionally, until it begins to brown — 10 to 12 minutes. Return the meat to the pan. Pour in the stock and white wine and, if necessary, enough water to raise the liquid level two thirds up the side of the meat. Bring the liquid to a simmer, cover the pan and braise the meat for 25 minutes. Turn the pieces and continue cooking them for 20 minutes.

Stir the carrot into the pan and cook it for 10 minutes. Whisk the cornflour mixture into the simmering liquid; stir constantly until the sauce thickens slightly. Serve the beef and fennel immediately.

SUGGESTED ACCOMPANIMENT: *lettuce and tomato salad.*

Roulades in Tomato Sauce

Serves 8
Working time: about 1 hour and 30 minutes
Total time: about 4 hours

Calories **235**
Protein **25g**
Cholesterol **55mg**
Total fat **8g**
Saturated fat **3g**
Sodium **165mg**

1 kg	topside of beef, trimmed of fat and cut on the diagonal into 16 slices	2 lb
1 tsp	safflower oil	1 tsp
3	onions, finely chopped	3
4	garlic cloves, finely chopped	4
2	carrots, finely chopped	2
1.5 kg	canned whole tomatoes, with their juice	3 lb
2	bay leaves	2
3 tbsp	chopped parsley	3 tbsp
2 tbsp	chopped fresh oregano, or 2 tsp dried oregano	2 tbsp
45 g	dry breadcrumbs	1½ oz
4 tbsp	freshly grated Parmesan cheese	4 tbsp
2 tbsp	finely chopped prosciutto or cooked ham	2 tbsp
4 tbsp	dry white wine	4 tbsp

Mix the oil, onions, garlic and carrots in a large, heavy-bottomed saucepan. Cover, and cook the mixture over low heat until the onions are translucent — about 15 minutes.

Purée the tomatoes in a food processor or a blender. Add the purée and bay leaves to the onion-and-carrot mixture. Increase the heat to medium and simmer the vegetables, uncovered, until they become a thick sauce — about 2 hours.

While the sauce is simmering, make the roulades. In a bowl, combine the parsley, oregano, breadcrumbs, cheese, prosciutto or ham, and the wine. Spread the beef slices flat on the work surface and spread some of the stuffing mixture on each one. Roll up each slice and tie it with two short pieces of string to secure it.

Add the roulades to the thickened sauce and simmer them until the meat is tender — about 1 hour. Lift the roulades from the sauce and remove the string. Spoon the sauce over the roulades and serve them immediately.

SUGGESTED ACCOMPANIMENT: *fettuccine.*

Cabbage Rolls with Beef and Sage

Serves 6
Working time: about 30 minutes
Total time: about 2 hours

Calories **305**
Protein **27g**
Cholesterol **60mg**
Total fat **9g**
Saturated fat **3g**
Sodium **250mg**

750 g	topside of beef, trimmed of fat and cut on the diagonal into 12 thin slices	1 ½ lb
1	large green cabbage (about 2 kg/4 lb)	1
1 tbsp	safflower oil	1 tbsp
350 g	onion, chopped	12 oz
1 tbsp	chopped fresh sage, or 1 tsp dried sage	1 tbsp
4	garlic cloves, finely chopped	4
3	slices white bread, crumbled	3
30 g	stemmed parsley sprigs	1 oz
800 g	canned whole tomatoes, crushed in their juice	1 ¾ lb
3	carrots, thinly sliced	3
3 tbsp	cider vinegar	3 tbsp
1 ½ tbsp	sugar	1 ½ tbsp
¼ tsp	salt	¼ tsp
	freshly ground black pepper	

Carefully remove 12 large outer leaves from the cabbage. Cut a small V-shaped wedge from each leaf to remove the tough core. Cook the leaves in a large pan of boiling water until they are translucent and limp — about 10 minutes. Drain the leaves in a colander.

Finely slice 450 g (15 oz) of the remaining cabbage. Save the rest for future use.

To prepare the filling, heat the oil in a large, heavy or non-stick frying pan over medium heat. Add the sliced cabbage, 275 g (9 oz) of the onion, 2 teaspoons of the fresh sage or ½ teaspoon of the dried sage, and half of the garlic. Cook the mixture, stirring occasionally, until the onion is translucent and the cabbage is soft — about 10 minutes. Transfer the mixture to a bowl, add the crumbled bread and the parsley, and toss well. Set the filling aside.

Meanwhile, put the tomatoes and their juice, the remaining garlic, the carrots and 17.5 cl (6 fl oz) of water into a very large frying pan. Cook the mixture, stirring occasionally, over low heat for 15 minutes. Add the remaining onion, the vinegar, the sugar, the remaining sage, the salt and some pepper. Allow the sauce to simmer slowly while you prepare the rolls.

With a meat bat or the flat of a heavy knife, pound the beef slices between two pieces of polythene to a thickness of 3 mm (⅛ inch). Sprinkle each of the slices with some black pepper.

Set a cabbage leaf on a work surface with the stem end towards you. Lay a beef slice on top of the leaf, then mound 2 heaped tablespoons of the filling on the beef. Roll up the leaf, starting at the stem end; fold in the sides over the filling as you go. Repeat the process with the remaining leaves, meat and filling.

Place the cabbage rolls, seam sides down, in the simmering sauce. Cook the rolls, with the pan lid slightly ajar, over low to medium-low heat for 1¼ hours. Carefully transfer the rolls to a platter. Spoon the sauce over them and serve immediately.

SUGGESTED ACCOMPANIMENT: *barley-mushroom pilaff.*

Braised Cinnamon Beef Roll

Serves 4
Working time: about 25 minutes
Total time: about 2 hours

Calories **250**
Protein **28g**
Cholesterol **70mg**
Total fat **11g**
Saturated fat **3g**
Sodium **215mg**

600 g	topside of beef, trimmed of fat and cut into four slices	1¼ lb
1 tbsp	ground cinnamon	1 tbsp
¼ tsp	salt	¼ tsp
	freshly ground black pepper	
1 tbsp	safflower oil	1 tbsp
1	large onion, thinly sliced	1
1	garlic clove, finely chopped	1
2	cinnamon sticks	2
12.5 cl	dry white wine	4 fl oz
¼ litre	unsalted brown or chicken stock (recipes, page 138)	8 fl oz
1 tbsp	cornflour, mixed with 1 tbsp of the stock	1 tbsp

Place the beef slices between two sheets of polythene or greaseproof paper and pound them with a meat bat or the flat of a heavy knife to a thickness of 3 mm (⅛ inch). Sprinkle the meat with the ground cinnamon, the salt and some pepper. Overlap the edges of two slices, spiced side up; cover the seam thus formed with polythene or greaseproof paper and lightly pound the overlapping edges to join the slices. Join the remaining two slices together by the same procedure.

Place one of the joined pieces on top of the other, again spiced side up, then roll them up tightly, starting with one of the longer edges. To hold the roll together, tie it with string *(page 25).*

Heat 1 teaspoon of the oil in a sauté pan over medium-high heat and sear the beef on all sides. Remove the meat; add the remaining 2 teaspoons of oil and the onion to the pan and cook the onion over medium heat, stirring occasionally, until it is translucent — 4 to 5 minutes. Stir in the garlic, cinnamon sticks, wine and stock. Return the beef to the pan and, if necessary, pour in enough water to half submerge the roll. Bring the liquid to a simmer, cover the pan

tightly, and continue simmering the roll until the meat feels tender when pierced with the tip of a sharp knife — 1¼ to 1½ hours.

When the beef roll is cooked, transfer it to a plate. Increase the heat to medium high and bring the liquid in the pan to the boil. Remove the cinnamon sticks and discard them. Whisk the cornflour paste into the liquid, whisking continuously until the sauce thickens — about 30 seconds.

Remove the string, slice the meat thinly, and place the slices on a warm serving platter. Top them with some of the sauce, pouring the rest round the beef. Serve immediately.

SUGGESTED ACCOMPANIMENT: *brown rice tossed with spring onions and raisins.*

atoes, the garlic, salt, peppercorns, bay leaf and thyme, and bring the liquid to the boil. Reduce the heat to low, cover the casserole, and simmer the beef until it feels very tender when pierced with a fork — 2 to 3 hours. Remove the pot roast from the casserole without discarding the cooking liquid; keep the roast warm.

Add the carrots, the celeriac or celery, the onions, and the parsnips or turnips to the cooking liquid. Simmer the vegetables until they are tender — approximately 20 minutes.

Cut the roast into slices and arrange them on a serving platter. Surround the meat with the vegetables. Spoon some of the cooking liquid over the meat and pour the rest into a sauce bowl to be passed separately.

Pot Roast with Parsnips

Serves 10
Working time: about 30 minutes
Total time: about 2 hours and 30 minutes

Calories **290**
Protein **33g**
Cholesterol **95mg**
Total fat **10g**
Saturated fat **3g**
Sodium **215mg**

1.75 kg	topside of beef or top rump, trimmed of fat	3½ lb
1 tbsp	safflower oil	1 tbsp
¼ litre	unsalted brown or chicken stock (recipes, page 138)	8 fl oz
400 g	canned tomatoes, puréed and strained	14 oz
2	garlic cloves, finely chopped	2
½ tsp	salt	½ tsp
10	black peppercorns, crushed	10
1	bay leaf	1
1 tbsp	chopped fresh thyme, or 1 tsp dried thyme	1 tbsp
3	carrots, peeled and cut on the diagonal into 1 cm (½ inch) thick ovals	3
350 g	celeriac, peeled and cut into 1 cm (½ inch) cubes, or 3 sticks celery, cut into 1 cm (½ inch) pieces	12 oz
5	small onions, peeled and halved crosswise	5
500 g	parsnips or turnips, peeled and cut into 1 cm (½ inch) pieces	1 lb

Heat the oil in a large fireproof casserole over medium-high heat. Add the joint and brown it on both sides — 1 to 2 minutes per side — then pour in the stock and enough water to cover the meat. Add the puréed tom-

Braised Steak with Onions

Serves 6
Working time: about 1 hour
Total time: about 2 hours and 30 minutes

Calories **175**
Protein **22g**
Cholesterol **50mg**
Total fat **5g**
Saturated fat **2g**
Sodium **195mg**

850 g	topside of beef, trimmed of fat and cut into six steaks	1¾ lb
2 tsp	safflower oil	2 tsp
2	large onions, thinly sliced	2
½ litre	red wine	16 fl oz
2	carrots, cut into bâtonnets	2
1	stick celery, chopped	1
¼ tsp	salt	¼ tsp
	freshly ground black pepper	
½ litre	unsalted brown stock or unsalted chicken stock (recipes, page 138)	16 fl oz

Preheat the oven to 170°C (325°F or Mark 3).

Heat the oil in a large, shallow fireproof casserole over medium heat. Add the onions and cook them, stirring frequently, until they are translucent and their juices have caramelized — 5 to 10 minutes. Pour 12.5 cl (4 fl oz) of the wine into the casserole, increase the heat and boil the wine until nearly all the liquid has evaporated. Pour in another 12.5 cl (4 fl oz) and reduce this also. Boil away the remaining wine in two batches, stirring constantly as the last batch begins to evaporate.

Add the carrots, celery, salt, some pepper and the stock to the casserole. Lay the steaks on top of the vegetables; cover the casserole and transfer it to the oven. Braise the steaks until they are tender — 1½ to 2 hours. Serve the steaks topped with the vegetables and braising juices.

SUGGESTED ACCOMPANIMENT: *potatoes and swedes mashed together and sprinkled with chopped parsley.*

Steak Braised in Spicy Vinegar Sauce

Serves 4
Working time: about 15 minutes
Total time: about 4 hours and 15 minutes
(includes marinating)

Calories **235**
Protein **28g**
Cholesterol **80mg**
Total fat **11g**
Saturated fat **3g**
Sodium **245mg**

600 g	sirloin steak, trimmed of fat and cut into four pieces	1¼ lb
1	garlic clove, finely chopped	1
1 tbsp	chopped fresh oregano, or 1 tsp dried oregano	1 tbsp
	hot red pepper flakes	
4 tbsp	balsamic vinegar, or 3 tbsp red wine vinegar mixed with 1 tsp honey	4 tbsp
1 tbsp	safflower oil	1 tbsp
¼ tsp	salt	¼ tsp
	freshly ground black pepper	
400 g	canned whole tomatoes, with their juice	14 oz
2 tbsp	freshly grated Parmesan cheese	2 tbsp
	parsley sprigs	

Put the pieces of meat into a shallow, non-reactive dish and add the garlic, oregano, a pinch of red pepper flakes and the vinegar. Let the meat marinate for 3 hours in the refrigerator. Drain the meat and pat the pieces dry, reserving the marinade.

Heat the oil in a large, heavy, fireproof casserole over medium-high heat. Sear the meat on both sides, then season it with the salt and some black pepper. Purée the tomatoes in a food processor or a blender and add them and the reserved marinade to the casserole. Cover it and simmer the meat in the sauce for 30 minutes. Turn the meat, replace the cover, and continue braising the pieces until they are tender — approximately 30 to 45 minutes.

Transfer the beef to a heated platter and spoon the sauce over it. Serve the dish topped with the grated cheese and garnished with parsley sprigs.

SUGGESTED ACCOMPANIMENTS: *pasta tossed with some of the spicy vinegar sauce; steamed courgettes.*

Red-Cooked Beef

Serves 6
Working time: about 30 minutes
Total time: about 2 hours and 30 minutes

Calories **270**
Protein **38g**
Cholesterol **75mg**
Total fat **8g**
Saturated fat **3g**
Sodium **105mg**

1 kg	topside of beef, trimmed of fat and cut into 2 cm (¾ inch) pieces	2 lb
4	Chinese dried mushrooms, soaked in hot water for 10 to 15 minutes	4
3 tbsp	low-sodium soy sauce or shoyu	3 tbsp
2 tbsp	dry sherry	2 tbsp
2 tbsp	soft brown sugar	2 tbsp
1 tbsp	tomato paste	1 tbsp
2.5 cm	fresh ginger root, peeled and crushed	1 inch
2	garlic cloves, crushed	2
½ tsp	five-spice powder	½ tsp
¼ litre	unsalted brown stock (recipe, page 138)	8 fl oz
1 tbsp	safflower oil	1 tbsp
300 g	carrots, thinly sliced diagonally	10 oz

Drain the mushrooms and gently squeeze out excess moisture. Trim and slice them. Place them in a bowl with the soy sauce or shoyu, sherry, brown sugar, tomato paste, ginger, garlic, five-spice powder and stock. Stir well and set aside.

Heat the oil in a heavy fireproof casserole over high heat. Add one third of the beef pieces and brown them on all sides, turning them constantly — about 5 minutes. With a slotted spoon, drain the meat, then transfer it to a plate lined with paper towels. Repeat with the remaining two batches of beef, draining each batch on fresh towels. Return all the beef to the casserole, add the mushrooms and liquid mixture and bring slowly to the boil. Reduce the heat, cover and simmer very gently for 1½ hours, turning the meat over frequently during this time and basting with the cooking liquid.

Add the carrots and continue cooking for a further 30 minutes or until the beef is tender; the carrots should be cooked but still firm. Serve hot.

SUGGESTED ACCOMPANIMENT: *stir-fried mange-tout and bean sprouts.*

Beef Daube Provençal

THIS LOW-FAT VERSION OF A FRENCH DAUBE USES
GRAPE JUICE IN THE MARINADE AND IS DELICIOUS REHEATED THE
FOLLOWING DAY.

Serves 6
Working time: about 1 hour
Total time: about 12 hours (includes marinating)

Calories **350**
Protein **37g**
Cholesterol **75mg**
Total fat **10g**
Saturated fat **3g**
Sodium **400mg**

750 g	beef topside, trimmed of fat and cut into 2.5 cm (1 inch) cubes	1½ lb
¼ litre	white grape juice	8 fl oz
12.5 cl	dry white wine	4 fl oz
2 tbsp	brandy	2 tbsp
1 tbsp	white wine vinegar	1 tbsp
250 g	onions, sliced	8 oz
250 g	carrots, sliced	8 oz
1	large garlic clove, chopped	1
1	bay leaf	1
1	fresh rosemary sprig	1
3 or 4	fresh thyme sprigs	3 or 4
2	large parsley sprigs	2
6	black peppercorns, lightly crushed	6
½ tsp	salt	½ tsp
2 to 3 tbsp	virgin olive oil	2 to 3 tbsp
1.25 kg	ripe tomatoes, skinned, seeded and chopped, or 800 g (28 oz) canned tomatoes, chopped	2½ lb
250 g	mushrooms, wiped and sliced	8 oz
1	strip pared orange rind	1
60 g	prosciutto, trimmed of excess fat and cut into strips	2 oz
12	black olives	12

In a large bowl, combine the grape juice, wine, brandy, vinegar, onions, carrots, garlic, herbs, peppercorns and salt. Add the beef and mix the ingredients together. Cover the bowl and leave in the refrigerator for 8 to 12 hours, stirring two or three times.

Preheat the oven to 150°C (300°F or Mark 2). Drain the meat, reserving the marinade, and pat the cubes dry with paper towels. Heat 1 tablespoon of the oil in a large, non-stick frying pan over high heat. Add about one third of the meat and cook until the pieces are well browned on all sides — 2 to 3 minutes. With a slotted spoon transfer the meat to a large fireproof casserole. Brown the remaining beef in two batches in the same way, adding more oil to the frying pan as necessary.

Pour the reserved marinade over the meat and add the chopped tomatoes, mushrooms and orange rind. Stir together. Bring the mixture to the boil, cover the casserole tightly and place it in the oven. Cook for 2½ hours.

Add the prosciutto and olives, and cook for a further 30 minutes or until the beef is very tender. If there is a lot of excess liquid at this stage, cook uncovered.

SUGGESTED ACCOMPANIMENT: *green salad.*

Spiced Chili Beef with Yogurt

THIS IS A VARIATION OF THE INDIAN CURRY ROGAN GOSHT. IT CAN BE
MADE A DAY IN ADVANCE AND REHEATED.

Serves 4
Working time: about 1 hour and 15 minutes
Total time: about 3 hours and 30 minutes

Calories **295**
Protein **40g**
Cholesterol **95mg**
Total fat **12g**
Saturated fat **6g**
Sodium **265mg**

600 g	topside of beef, trimmed of fat and cut into 2 cm (¾ inch) cubes	1¼ lb
6	cardamom pods	6
2 tsp	coriander seeds	2 tsp
2 tsp	cumin seeds	2 tsp
30 g	ghee or clarified butter, or 2 tbsp safflower oil	1 oz
1	medium onion, finely chopped	1
2	garlic cloves, crushed	2
2	fresh green chili peppers, finely chopped (caution, page 8)	2
2.5 cm	fresh ginger root, peeled and crushed	1 inch
2 tsp	ground turmeric	2 tsp
500 g	tomatoes, skinned and coarsely chopped	1 lb
¼ tsp	salt	¼ tsp
17.5 cl	plain low-fat yogurt (at room temperature)	6 fl oz
½	small sweet red pepper, seeded, deribbed and sliced into rings	½
½	small sweet green pepper, seeded, deribbed and sliced into rings	½

Split the cardamom pods open and remove the seeds.
Put the seeds in a heavy pan with the coriander and
cumin seeds over moderate heat. Dry-fry for about 5
minutes, shaking the pan constantly until the seeds

give off a spicy aroma. Remove from the pan and crush with a mortar and pestle. Set aside.

Melt half the ghee, butter or oil in a fireproof casserole, add one third of the beef pieces and brown them on all sides over high heat, turning them constantly — about 5 minutes. With a slotted spoon, drain the beef and transfer it to a plate lined with paper towels. Repeat with the remaining two batches of beef, draining each batch on fresh towels.

Lower the heat and add the onion, garlic, chili peppers and ginger to the casserole, stirring to scrape up the sediment from the bottom. Cook gently, stirring constantly, until softened but not browned — 5 to 8 minutes. Meanwhile, preheat the oven to 150°C (300°F or Mark 2).

Add the crushed spices and turmeric, and cook, stirring, for a further 2 minutes. Increase the heat, then add the tomatoes and salt, and cook, stirring, for 5 minutes. Return the beef to the casserole and stir well to mix evenly with the other ingredients.

Reserve about 3 tablespoons of yogurt. Add the remainder to the casserole, 1 tablespoon at a time. Stir-fry after each addition until the yogurt is absorbed before adding the next spoonful — otherwise it will curdle. Cover the casserole with a double thickness of greaseproof paper or foil and a lid. Cook in the oven for 2 hours until the meat is tender, stirring occasionally.

Just before serving, melt the remaining ghee, butter or oil in a heavy frying pan over moderately high heat, add the pepper rings and toss for 2 to 3 minutes until softened slightly. Drain on paper towels. Transfer the contents of the casserole to a warmed serving dish, top with the pepper rings and dribble with the reserved yogurt. Serve hot.

SUGGESTED ACCOMPANIMENTS: *naan bread; spinach.*

Spicy Beef Stew with Apricots and Olives

Serves 8
Working time: about 30 minutes
Total time: about 2 hours and 30 minutes

Calories **290**
Protein **29g**
Cholesterol **70mg**
Total fat **11g**
Saturated fat **3g**
Sodium **275mg**

1.25 kg	topside of beef, trimmed of fat and cut into 4 cm (1½ inch) cubes	2½ lb
1 tbsp	safflower oil	1 tbsp
3	onions, chopped	3
4	garlic cloves, finely chopped	4
400 g	canned whole tomatoes, chopped, with their juice	14 oz
½ litre	unsalted brown or chicken stock (recipes, page 138)	16 fl oz
12.5 cl	red wine	4 fl oz
1½ tsp	ground cumin	1½ tsp
1½ tsp	ground coriander	1½ tsp
⅛ tsp	cayenne pepper	⅛ tsp
125 g	dried apricots, halved	4 oz
16	green olives, stoned, rinsed and drained	16

Heat the oil in a large, heavy frying pan over medium heat. Add the onions and cook them, stirring often, until translucent — about 5 minutes. With a slotted spoon, transfer the onions to a fireproof casserole.

Increase the heat to medium high. Add the beef cubes to the frying pan and brown them on all sides — 5 to 7 minutes.

Transfer the beef to the casserole and add the garlic, the tomatoes and their juice, the stock, wine, cumin, coriander and cayenne pepper. Cover the casserole and reduce the heat to low; simmer the beef, stirring occasionally, for 1½ hours.

Stir the apricots and olives into the casserole, and continue cooking the stew until the meat is tender — about 30 minutes more. Transfer the stew to a bowl or a deep platter, and serve.

SUGGESTED ACCOMPANIMENT: *rice tossed with spring onions, currants and sweet red pepper.*

Bollito Misto

THIS LIGHTER VERSION OF THE CLASSIC ITALIAN BOILED DINNER
CALLS FOR COOKING THE BEEF GENTLY FOR A LONG TIME. IF YOU
LIKE, THE DISH MAY BE PREPARED IN ADVANCE AND REHEATED.

Serves 16
Working time: about 1 hour and 15 minutes
Total time: about 6 hours

Calories **280**
Protein **33g**
Cholesterol **90mg**
Total fat **9g**
Saturated fat **3g**
Sodium **220mg**

2 kg	rump or topside of beef, trimmed of fat	4 lb
1.5 kg	chicken	3 lb
16	carrots, cut into 6 cm (2½ inch) lengths	16
10	sticks celery, cut into 6 cm (2½ inch) lengths	10
2	onions, quartered	2
2	bay leaves	2
8	peppercorns	8
2	fresh thyme sprigs, or ½ tsp dried thyme	2
2	unpeeled garlic cloves	2
16	small white onions, peeled	16
Red sauce		
800 g	canned whole tomatoes, with their juice	1¾ lb
1	onion, finely chopped	1
3 tbsp	cider vinegar	3 tbsp
4 tbsp	dry breadcrumbs	4 tbsp
¼ tsp	hot red pepper flakes	¼ tsp
Green sauce		
75 g	dry breadcrumbs	2½ oz
2 tsp	capers, rinsed	2 tsp
2 tbsp	chopped parsley	2 tbsp
3	garlic cloves	3
2	anchovies, rinsed and patted dry	2

Put the beef, one quarter each of the carrots and celery, the quartered onions, bay leaves, peppercorns, thyme and garlic into a large pan. Pour in enough water to cover them; bring to a simmer over medium-low heat. Simmer the beef and vegetables for 3 hours.

Add the chicken to the pan and, if necessary, enough water to cover it. Continue to simmer the mixture until the chicken is tender and its juices run clear when a thigh is pierced with the tip of a sharp knife — about 45 minutes. Remove the beef and chicken from the pan and set them aside. Reserve the broth.

Meanwhile, make the sauces. For the red sauce, purée the tomatoes in a food processor or a blender. Strain the purée into a non-reactive saucepan, and add the onion, vinegar, breadcrumbs and pepper flakes. Simmer the mixture, stirring occasionally, for 45 minutes. Pour the sauce into a bowl and refrigerate it.

For the green sauce, purée the breadcrumbs, capers, parsley, garlic, anchovies and 17.5 cl (6 fl oz) of the broth from the pan in a food processor or a blender. Pour the sauce into a small bowl and refrigerate it.

Skim the fat from the broth. Strain the broth through a sieve lined with muslin into a bowl; discard the solids. Rinse out the pan, then pour the broth back into it. Add the remaining carrots and celery, and the white onions. Simmer the vegetables until they are tender — 20 to 30 minutes.

Return the beef and chicken to the pan, cover the pan, and simmer them until they are heated through — about 15 minutes. Carve the beef and chicken, discard-ing the chicken skin. Arrange the pieces on a warm serving platter and moisten them with some of the broth. Save the rest of the broth for future use. Place the vegetables around the meat and serve immediately, with the sauces passed in separate bowls.

SUGGESTED ACCOMPANIMENT: *green salad.*

Japanese Simmered Beef

THIS DISH IS A MEAL IN ITSELF. TRADITIONALLY, THE INGREDIENTS ARE PREPARED AND COOKED AT THE TABLE.

Serves 6
Working time: about 25 minutes
Total time: about 40 minutes

Calories **230**
Protein **20g**
Cholesterol **35mg**
Total fat **7g**
Saturated fat **2g**
Sodium **350mg**

500 g	beef fillet, trimmed of fat and thinly sliced against the grain	1 lb
125 g	Japanese udon noodles or vermicelli	4 oz
1	large carrot, thinly sliced on the diagonal	1
60 g	shiitake or other fresh mushrooms, wiped clean, the stems discarded and the caps thinly sliced	2 oz
3	spring onions, julienned	3
90 g	Chinese cabbage, cut into chiffonade	3 oz
250 g	tofu, cut into 2 cm (¾ inch) wide strips	8 oz
1.5 litres	unsalted brown or chicken stock (recipes, page 138), or a combination of both	2½ pints
2 tbsp	low-sodium soy sauce or shoyu	2 tbsp
2 tbsp	rice vinegar	2 tbsp
1 tsp	finely chopped fresh ginger root	1 tsp
1 tsp	finely chopped garlic	1 tsp
¼ tsp	dark sesame oil	¼ tsp

Precook the noodles or vermicelli in 2 litres (3½ pints) of boiling water. Begin testing for doneness after 8 minutes and cook them until they are *al dente.* Drain the noodles in a colander and rinse them under running water to keep them from sticking together. Drain them again and set them aside in a bowl.

Arrange the beef slices, the vegetables and the tofu on a large plate.

Combine the stock, soy sauce, vinegar, ginger and garlic in an electric frying pan, a wok or a fondue pot. Bring the mixture to a simmer and cook it for 5 minutes, then add the sesame oil.

Begin the meal by cooking pieces of the beef briefly in the simmering broth — 30 seconds to 1 minute. After the meat has been eaten, cook the vegetables and tofu in the broth just until they are warmed through — 3 to 4 minutes. Finish the meal with the noodles or vermicelli, adding them to the broth and heating them. They may be eaten with the broth or served on their own.

Fruit-Stuffed Veal Olives

Serves 4
Working time: about 45 minutes
Total time: about 1 hour and 5 minutes

Calories **185**
Protein **18g**
Cholesterol **80mg**
Total fat **6g**
Saturated fat **1g**
Sodium **200mg**

4	veal escalopes (about 90 g/3 oz each), trimmed of fat and flattened (page 32, Step 1)	4
1 tbsp	safflower oil	1 tbsp
About 15 cl	red grape juice	About ¼ pint
½ tbsp	arrowroot	½ tbsp
	red apples, sliced	
	seedless green grapes	
	Spiced fruit stuffing	
60 g	fresh cranberries, or frozen cranberries, thawed	2 oz
1	crisp eating apple (about 150 g/5 oz), quartered and cored	1
75 g	seedless green grapes	2½ oz
1½ tsp	freshly grated ginger root	1½ tsp
½ tsp	mixed spice	½ tsp
½ tsp	salt	½ tsp
	freshly ground black pepper	

First make the stuffing. Put the cranberries, apple quarters, grapes and ginger in a food processor and blend until quite fine. Drain the fruit mixture in a fine sieve placed over a bowl to catch the juice, pressing down on the fruit to squeeze out all excess liquid; reserve the liquid. Add the mixed spice, salt and some pepper to the fruit mixture and stir to blend. Spread one quarter of the fruit mixture over each escalope, then roll them up, tucking in the sides. Tie each roll with string.

Heat the oil in a small, non-stick frying pan over medium-high heat. Add the veal rolls and brown them on all sides — about 5 minutes. As they are browned, transfer them to a saucepan in which they will fit comfortably. Add enough grape juice to the reserved fruit juice to make 30 cl (½ pint). Pour this over the rolls and bring to the boil. Reduce the heat, cover and simmer for 20 minutes, turning the rolls after 10 minutes.

Transfer the veal rolls to a warmed dish, slice them and keep hot. Mix the arrowroot with a little cold water to make a smooth paste, then stir it into the cooking liquid. Simmer, stirring constantly, until it has thickened. Pour the sauce around the veal rolls and garnish with apple slices and grapes. Serve hot.

SUGGESTED ACCOMPANIMENT: *French beans.*

Milanese-Style Braised Veal

Serves 6
Working time: about 40 minutes
Total time: about 2 hours and 45 minutes

Calories **290**
Protein **20g**
Cholesterol **75mg**
Total fat **10g**
Saturated fat **3g**
Sodium **210mg**

600 g	topside of veal, trimmed of fat and cut into 2 cm (¾ inch) pieces	1¼ lb
2 tbsp	virgin olive oil	2 tbsp
3	carrots, coarsely chopped	3
2	sticks celery, trimmed and coarsely chopped	2
1	onion, finely chopped	1
2	garlic cloves, one crushed, one chopped	2
1.25 kg	ripe tomatoes, skinned, seeded and chopped, or 800 g (28 oz) canned plum tomatoes	2½ lb
8 cl	dry white wine	3 fl oz
2	bay leaves	2
2	strips of lemon rind	2
3 tbsp	finely chopped fresh mixed herbs (parsley, oregano, thyme)	3 tbsp
¼ tsp	salt	¼ tsp
	freshly ground black pepper	
1	lemon, grated rind only	1

Heat 1 tablespoon of the oil in a fireproof casserole over high heat, add one third of the veal and brown the pieces on all sides, turning them constantly — about 5 minutes. With a slotted spoon, transfer the meat to a plate lined with paper towels. Repeat with the remaining two batches of veal, draining each batch on fresh towels.

Add the remaining oil to the casserole and lower the heat. Add the carrots, celery and onion to the casserole, stirring to scrape up the sediment from the bottom of the pan, and sweat the vegetables over the ▶

lowest possible heat for 10 minutes. Preheat the oven to 150°C (300°F or Mark 2).

Uncover the casserole and add the crushed garlic, the veal, tomatoes, wine, bay leaves, strips of lemon rind, 1 tablespoon of the mixed herbs, the salt and some pepper. Bring slowly to the boil, stirring, then cover with greaseproof paper or foil and a lid. Braise the meat in the oven for 2 hours, or until the meat is tender, stirring occasionally to ensure even cooking.

Before serving, mix together the chopped garlic, remaining herbs and the grated lemon rind. Remove the bay leaves and strips of lemon rind from the casserole, transfer the contents of the casserole to a warmed serving dish and sprinkle the garlic, herb and lemon mixture over the top. Serve hot.

SUGGESTED ACCOMPANIMENT: *saffron rice.*

EDITOR'S NOTE: *This dish benefits from being left to stand overnight and reheated before serving. The flavours mellow and mature beautifully during this time.*

Italian Veal with Tuna Sauce Italian-Style

THIS RECIPE IS BASED ON THE CLASSIC VITELLO TONNATO.
TOFU IS USED TO GIVE A SMOOTH, LOW-FAT SAUCE.

Serves 6
Working time: about 50 minutes
Total time: about 1 day and 5 hours (includes chilling)

Calories **270**
Protein **40g**
Cholesterol **135mg**
Total fat **10g**
Saturated fat **3g**
Sodium **260mg**

1.25 kg	loin of veal, boned, trimmed of fat, rolled and tied	2½ lb
1	carrot, sliced	1
1	stick celery, sliced	1
1	onion, sliced	1
1 to 2	bay leaves	1 to 2
	fresh rosemary and thyme sprigs	
1	small bunch parsley, tied with string	1
8	black peppercorns	8
⅛ tsp	salt	⅛ tsp
¾ litre	unsalted chicken or veal stock (recipes, page 138)	1¼ pints
Tuna sauce		
300 g	silken tofu (bean curd), drained	10 oz
1 tbsp	virgin olive oil	1 tbsp
2 tbsp	fresh lemon juice	2 tbsp
2	garlic cloves, crushed	2
¼ tsp	white pepper	¼ tsp
100 g	canned tuna in brine, drained and finely flaked	3½ oz
Garnish		
60 g	canned anchovy fillets, soaked in 6 tbsp milk for 20 minutes, drained, rinsed and patted dry	2 oz
1 to 2 tbsp	capers, drained	1 to 2 tbsp

Put the carrot, celery and onion in the bottom of a heavy fireproof casserole. Add the bay leaves, rosemary, thyme, parsley, peppercorns and salt, then place the veal on top. Pour the stock round the meat and bring the liquid slowly to the boil. Reduce the heat, cover the casserole and poach gently until the veal feels tender when pierced in the centre with a skewer — about 1½ hours. Remove the casserole from the heat and leave it covered in a cold place until the veal has cooled in the liquid.

Transfer the veal to a cutting board. Strain the stock into a bowl and return half the liquid to the rinsed-out pan (reserve the rest for another use). Bring to the boil and boil vigorously until the liquid has reduced to 4 tablespoons — 5 to 8 minutes. Set aside to cool. Carve the meat into 12 neat slices and arrange them on a serving platter. Cover loosely with foil and set aside in a cold place.

To make the tuna sauce, purée the tofu in a blender or food processor with the oil, lemon juice, garlic and white pepper. Add the tuna and the reduced cooking liquid and process the mixture until it has a smooth, coating consistency. Uncover the veal and coat it with the sauce, making sure that all the meat is covered. Cover the platter loosely with foil and chill in the refrigerator for 24 hours, to allow the flavour of the sauce to permeate the meat.

Remove the veal from the refrigerator about 30 minutes before serving. Decorate it with the anchovies and capers.

SUGGESTED ACCOMPANIMENTS: *granary bread; tomato and black olive salad.*

Blanquette of Veal

Serves 4
Working time: about 50 minutes
Total time: about 2 hours

Calories **190**
Protein **20g**
Cholesterol **125mg**
Total fat **7g**
Saturated fat **3g**
Sodium **250mg**

350 g	topside of veal or top rump, trimmed of fat and cut into 2.5 cm (1 inch) cubes	12 oz
8	pearl onions or shallots	8
8	button mushrooms, wiped clean	8
1	stick celery, cut into chunks	1
1	fresh thyme sprig, or ½ tsp dried thyme	1
1	bay leaf	1
2	parsley sprigs	2
60 cl	unsalted veal or chicken stock (recipes, page 138)	1 pint
8	small carrots	8
1 tbsp	cornflour	1 tbsp
¼ litre	semi-skimmed milk	8 fl oz
1	egg yolk	1
1 tbsp	lemon juice	1 tbsp
½ tsp	salt	½ tsp
	white pepper	

Put the veal into a heavy, medium-sized saucepan and cover with cold water. Bring to the boil, then drain. Return the veal to the pan and add the onions, mushrooms, celery, thyme, bay leaf, parsley sprigs and stock. Bring to the boil, reduce the heat, cover and simmer for 25 minutes. Add the carrots and simmer for a further 20 minutes. Remove the veal and vegetables with a slotted spoon and set aside. Discard the herbs and strain the stock into a clean pan. Boil to reduce to 30 cl (½ pint) — 10 to 15 minutes.

Dissolve the cornflour in a little of the milk. Add the remaining milk to the stock and bring back to the boil.

Reduce the heat, whisk in the cornflour mixture and simmer for 10 minutes, stirring. Lightly beat the egg yolk with the lemon juice in a small bowl. Stir in a little of the hot sauce and stir this into the remaining sauce in the pan. Cook gently, stirring, for 1 minute. Add the salt and some white pepper. Return the veal and vegetables to the sauce and heat through gently without boiling. Serve hot.

SUGGESTED ACCOMPANIMENTS: *boiled rice; peas.*

Braised Veal

Serves 8
Working time: about 40 minutes
Total time: about 2 hours and 40 minutes

Calories **305**
Protein **33g**
Cholesterol **90mg**
Total fat **8g**
Saturated fat **3g**
Sodium **210mg**

1 kg	topside of veal, trimmed of fat and neatly tied	2 to 2½ lb
1 tbsp	virgin olive oil	1 tbsp
2	onions, sliced	2
4	carrots, coarsely sliced	4
3	sticks celery, coarsely sliced	3
1	leek, trimmed and coarsely sliced	1
250 g	swedes, diced	8 oz
2	garlic cloves	2
2	bay leaves	2
	rosemary sprigs	
	parsley sprigs	
1 tbsp	fresh thyme, or 1 tsp dried thyme	1 tbsp
¼ tsp	salt	¼ tsp
30 cl	unsalted veal or chicken stock (recipes, page 138)	½ pint
15 cl	dry white wine	¼ pint

Preheat the oven to 180°C (350°F or Mark 4).

Heat the oil in a large, heavy frying pan over high heat. Brown the veal on all sides — about 5 minutes. Remove the joint from the pan and set aside. Reduce the heat, add the onions, carrots, celery, leek and swedes to the oil remaining in the pan and toss them gently until they glisten. Add the stock and wine, and bring to the boil. Transfer the vegetables and stock to an ovenproof casserole, place the veal on top of the vegetables and add the garlic, bay leaves, rosemary, parsley, thyme and salt. Cover the casserole with a tight-fitting lid or foil.

Braise the veal in the oven for about 2 hours, basting frequently, until tender. When cooked *(below)*, transfer the veal to a hot serving dish, remove the string and cut into slices. Discard the bay leaves and herbs. Using a slotted spoon, lift two thirds of the vegetables, particularly the larger pieces, on to the serving dish. Cover and keep hot. Using a masher, mash the vegetables remaining in the stock. Bring to the boil, then pour into a hot serving jug or bowl. Serve with the veal.

SUGGESTED ACCOMPANIMENT: *creamed potatoes.*

Tagine of Veal with Dried Fruits and Pine-Nuts

TAGINE IS THE MOROCCAN WORD FOR AN EARTHENWARE COOKING POT — EXCELLENT FOR SLOW, MOIST OVEN COOKING, ESPECIALLY LEAN CUTS. FOR A SIMILAR EFFECT, YOU CAN USE AN ORDINARY CASSEROLE AND SEAL THE LID WITH A PASTE OF FLOUR AND WATER.

Serves 4
Working time: about 10 minutes
Total time: about 2 hours and 15 minutes

Calories **310**
Protein **29g**
Cholesterol **75mg**
Total fat **10g**
Saturated fat **2g**
Sodium **190mg**

600 g	topside of veal, trimmed of fat and cut into 2 cm (¾ inch) cubes	1 ¼ lb
½	large onion, finely chopped	½
2 ½ tsp	ground paprika	2 ½ tsp
1 ½ tsp	ground ginger	1 ½ tsp
½ tsp	ground cinnamon	½ tsp
	freshly ground black pepper	
⅛ tsp	salt	⅛ tsp
125 g	dried apricots	4 oz
125 g	prunes	4 oz
30 g	pine-nuts	1 oz
⅛ tsp	saffron threads	⅛ tsp
40 cl	unsalted chicken or veal stock (recipes, page 138)	¾ pint
	fresh coriander sprigs for garnish	

Preheat the oven to 170°C (325°F or Mark 3). In a large bowl, mix the veal, onion, paprika, ginger, cinnamon, some pepper and the salt, until the meat is evenly coated. Add the dried fruit and pine-nuts, then transfer the mixture to the cooking pot.

Bring the stock to the boil and stir in the saffron. Pour it over the meat mixture, cover and cook in the oven for 2 hours. Serve hot, straight from the pot, garnished with coriander.

SUGGESTED ACCOMPANIMENTS: *burghul; plain yogurt.*

Persian Veal and Bean Stew with Parsley

Serves 4
Working time: about 45 minutes
Total time: about 10 hours and 15 minutes
(includes soaking)

Calories **415**			
Protein **35g**	350 g	topside of veal or top rump, trimmed of fat and minced (page 15)	12 oz
Cholesterol **105mg**	125 g	dried chick-peas, soaked for 8 hours or overnight, drained	4 oz
Total fat **15g**			
Saturated fat **3g**	125 g	dried red kidney beans, soaked for 8 hours or overnight, drained	4 oz
Sodium **400mg**			
	2 tbsp	safflower oil	2 tbsp
	1	large onion, chopped	1
	1	garlic clove, finely chopped	1
	2	sticks celery, sliced	2
	90 g	parsley, stems removed, chopped	3 oz
	4 tbsp	lemon juice	4 tbsp
	45 cl	unsalted veal or chicken stock (recipes, page 138)	¾ pint
	1 tsp	ground allspice	1 tsp
	30 g	fresh wholemeal breadcrumbs	1 oz
	½ tsp	salt	½ tsp
		freshly ground black pepper	
	½	egg, beaten	½

Put the chick-peas and kidney beans in separate saucepans and cover with fresh cold water. Bring to the boil and boil for 10 minutes. Drain and set aside.

Heat 1 tablespoon of the oil in a 30 cm (12 inch) diameter, shallow, fireproof casserole. Add the onion, garlic, celery and 60 g (2 oz) of the parsley. Cover and cook gently, stirring occasionally, for about 10 minutes or until the vegetables are softened. Add the chick-peas, lemon juice, half the stock and the allspice and stir to mix. Bring to the boil, cover again and simmer for 30 minutes. Stir in the kidney beans with half the remaining stock. Cover again and simmer for 30 minutes.

Meanwhile, combine the veal, breadcrumbs, remaining parsley, half the salt and some pepper in a bowl. Work together with your hands, and add enough egg to bind. Divide into 12 equal portions and shape into balls. Heat the remaining oil in a non-stick frying pan over medium-high heat. Add the meatballs and brown on all sides, turning them and shaking the pan so that they colour evenly — about 5 minutes.

Add the meatballs to the bean stew. Add the remaining salt and some pepper. Simmer, covered, for a further 1 hour or until the beans are tender, stirring occasionally and adding a little extra stock if necessary.

SUGGESTED ACCOMPANIMENT: *chicory and orange salad.*

4 A phyllo parcel, baked to a rich gold, is sliced to reveal the beef fillet within (recipe, opposite).

A Medley of Ideas

Fillet of Beef Wrapped in Phyllo

Many of the new, light beef and veal dishes do not fall neatly into the traditional categories of roasting, grilling, frying or braising. This chapter rounds up an array of dishes, from barbecue to pâté, that reveals the range of opportunities open to the imaginative health-conscious cook.

Some of the recipes call for minced beef or veal, long the basis of many familiar dishes prepared on a family budget. However, the fatty meat usually minced by the supermarket is replaced with the leanest cuts, custom-minced by the butcher. Thus, the fat content stays low while the economical, meat-stretching appeal of such favourites as meat loaf and stuffed peppers is retained with the use of savoury vegetable and grain fillers.

In many of the dishes, the meat and its complementary spices, herbs or vegetables are sautéed together, then baked with other ingredients. This combination of techniques is one of the kitchen's happiest marriages, adding the flavour contributed by browning to the handsome appearance of a baked dish. On page 116 for example, minced beef is precooked with tomatoes, onion, green pepper and spices, then baked over a cornbread batter that rises to surround the meat in a tender, golden crust.

Baked dishes provide inspired contrasts and combinations: fillet of beef wrapped in phyllo (right); silky mashed potatoes covering beef cooked with shallots and apples (page 112); or beef cooked in a yogurt and egg custard garnished with almonds (page 119). And baking can transform minced or diced veal into dishes of great refinement; both the veal pâté with peaches and peppercorns (page 120) and the veal terrine with spinach, cheese and juniper (page 122) would make an excellent first course for a lunch or dinner party. As with all the recipes in the chapter, the calorie and fat content are moderate, yet flavour and texture have not been compromised.

Serves 8
Working time: about 40 minutes
Total time: about 3 hours and 15 minutes

Calories **300**
Protein **32g**
Cholesterol **65mg**
Total fat **12g**
Saturated fat **4g**
Sodium **75mg**

1 kg	beef fillet, fully trimmed and tied neatly	2½ lb
3 tbsp	virgin olive oil	3 tbsp
1 tsp	mixed dried herbs	1 tsp
1	garlic clove, crushed	1
	freshly ground black pepper	
4 tbsp	red wine	4 tbsp
1	onion, finely chopped	1
250 g	button mushrooms, trimmed and chopped	8 oz
2 tbsp	chopped parsley	2 tbsp
200 g	phyllo pastry (about 7 sheets, 30 by 45 cm/12 by 18 inches)	7 oz
15 g	butter, melted	½ oz
	cooked mushrooms to garnish (optional)	

In a shallow dish, blend 1 tablespoon of the oil with the herbs, garlic and pepper. Add the beef and turn it in the marinade until evenly coated. Cover and marinate at room temperature for at least 1 hour.

Heat another tablespoon of the oil in a non-stick sauté pan or frying pan over high heat. Brown the beef on all sides — about 5 to 8 minutes — then transfer it to a plate. Strain off all the fat from the pan and stir in 2 tablespoons of the wine. Bring to the boil and boil until reduced by half — about 1 minute. Pour over the beef and set the meat aside until cold.

Meanwhile, heat the remaining oil in the pan over medium heat, add the onion and cook gently for 5 to 6 minutes until softened, but not browned. Add the mushrooms and cook until they are softened — 6 to 8 minutes. Stir the remaining wine into the mushrooms, bring to the boil and cook until all the juices in the pan have evaporated — about 5 minutes. Stir in the parsley. Set aside to cool.

Heat the oven to 230°C (450°F or Mark 8). Lay the phyllo pastry sheets out flat, one on top of another, and cut a 5 cm (2 inch) wide strip from one side. Cut it into diamond shapes (Step 1, overleaf). Fill the phyllo with the mushroom mixture and beef fillet and make a neat parcel as illustrated overleaf.

Bake for 35 minutes until golden-brown. Carefully remove to a serving dish and garnish with the mushrooms. Cut into thick slices and serve immediately.

SUGGESTED ACCOMPANIMENT: *new potatoes with chives.*

Making a Light Pastry Parcel

1 *PREPARING THE DECORATION. Take seven 30 by 45 cm (12 by 18 inch) sheets of phyllo pastry and stack them on top of each other on a flat surface. With a sharp knife, trim off two 5 cm (2 inch) strips from one short side (below, left). Cut across the strips diagonally to make diamond shapes (below, right). Set the pieces aside for use later as decoration.*

2 *ASSEMBLING THE PARCEL. Spread the mushroom mixture lengthwise down the centre of the phyllo to form a rectangle approximately the length and width of the beef fillet. Cut the string from the fillet and lay the meat on top of the mushroom mixture. Fold the short sides of the phyllo over the ends of the beef.*

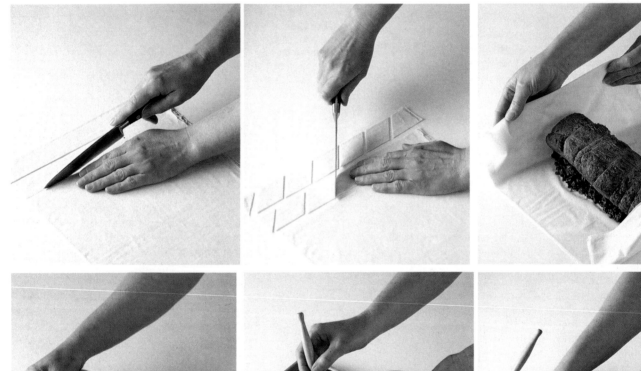

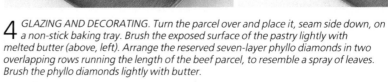

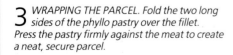

3 *WRAPPING THE PARCEL. Fold the two long sides of the phyllo pastry over the fillet. Press the pastry firmly against the meat to create a neat, secure parcel.*

4 *GLAZING AND DECORATING. Turn the parcel over and place it, seam side down, on a non-stick baking tray. Brush the exposed surface of the pastry lightly with melted butter (above, left). Arrange the reserved seven-layer phyllo diamonds in two overlapping rows running the length of the beef parcel, to resemble a spray of leaves. Brush the phyllo diamonds lightly with butter.*

Sirloin-Filled Pitta Sandwiches

Serves 6
Working (and total) time: about 1 hour and 15 minutes

Calories **300**
Protein **22g**
Cholesterol **40mg**
Total fat **11g**
Saturated fat **3g**
Sodium **205mg**

350 g	sirloin steak, trimmed of fat and thinly sliced	12 oz
1	red onion, thickly sliced	1
6	wholemeal pitta breads	6
125 g	low-fat mozzarella cheese, grated	4 oz
3	garlic cloves, finely chopped	3
12	Kalamata olives or black olives, stoned and chopped	12
2	large ripe tomatoes, each cut into six slices	2
1 tbsp	safflower oil	1 tbsp

Put the onion slices on the rack of a grill pan and grill them until they are soft — about 4 minutes. Remove the onions from the rack and set them aside. Lay the slices of meat on the rack and grill them until they are browned — about 2 minutes.

Split a pitta bread into two rounds. On the bottom half, layer one sixth of the onion, beef, cheese, garlic, olives and tomatoes. Set the top half in place. Repeat the process to make five more sandwiches.

Lightly brush the outside of the sandwiches with the oil. Toast the sandwiches in a waffle iron or in a frying pan over medium heat until the bread is crisp and brown and the cheese has melted —about 4 minutes. Cut each sandwich in two before serving.

Beef and Potato Pie

Serves 4
Working time: about 1 hour
Total time: about 2 hours

Calories **485** Protein **32g** Cholesterol **70mg** Total fat **12g** Saturated fat **3g** Sodium **270mg**			

600 g	topside of beef, trimmed of fat and minced (box, page 15)	1¼ lb
1 kg	potatoes, peeled and quartered	2 lb
2 tbsp	skimmed milk	2 tbsp
2 tbsp	chopped parsley	2 tbsp
¼ tsp	salt	¼ tsp
4 tsp	safflower oil	4 tsp
3 tbsp	plain flour	3 tbsp
½ litre	unsalted brown or chicken stock (recipes, page 138)	16 fl oz
115 g	shallots or onions, thinly sliced	4 oz
90 g	dried apples, chopped	3 oz
2 tbsp	cider vinegar	2 tbsp
1 tbsp	fresh thyme, or 1 tsp dried thyme	1 tbsp
	freshly ground black pepper	

Preheat the oven to 230°C (450°F or Mark 8).

Place the potatoes in a saucepan and add enough water to cover them. Bring the water to the boil, then reduce the heat, and simmer the potatoes until they are tender — 15 to 20 minutes. Drain the potatoes, spread them out on a baking sheet, and place them in the oven to dry. After 5 minutes, remove the pan from the oven and purée the potatoes by working them through a sieve or a food mill set over a bowl. Combine the potatoes with the milk, chopped parsley and salt and set them aside.

Blend 2 teaspoons of the oil and the flour in a saucepan over low heat and cook the paste for 1 minute. Gradually whisk in the stock and simmer the mixture slowly over low heat until it thickens — about 2

Beetroot Beefburgers

Serves 8
Working time: about 20 minutes
Total time: about 2 hours

Calories **320** Protein **31g** Cholesterol **70mg** Total fat **10g** Saturated fat **3g** Sodium **310mg**			

1.25 kg	topside of beef, trimmed of fat and minced (box, page 15)	2½ lb
1 kg	beetroots, washed, all but 2.5 cm (1 inch) of the stems cut off	2 lb
1	small onion, peeled and grated	1
8	cornichons, chopped, or 2 small gherkins, chopped	8
4 tbsp	dry breadcrumbs	4 tbsp
4 tbsp	distilled white vinegar	4 tbsp
	freshly ground black pepper	
2 tsp	safflower oil	2 tsp
12.5 cl	unsalted brown or chicken stock (recipes, page 138)	4 fl oz
1 tsp	caraway seeds	1 tsp
8	hamburger buns or baps, split	8

Preheat the oven to 200°C (400°F or Mark 6). Wrap all the beetroots together in a single package of aluminium foil and bake them until they are tender — approximately 1 hour. Unwrap them and let them cool. Peel and grate the beetroots. Put 90 g (3 oz) of the beetroot into a bowl, and set the remainder aside.

Add the minced beef, onion, cornichons or gherkins, breadcrumbs, vinegar and some pepper to the bowl. Mix the ingredients thoroughly, then shape the mixture into eight patties.

Heat the oil in a large, non-stick frying pan over medium-high heat. Add the patties to the pan and brown them for about 1 minute per side. Add the reserved beetroot, the stock, caraway seeds and some pepper. Cover the pan and reduce the heat to medium low. Simmer the mixture for 20 minutes.

Serve the beefburgers in the buns or baps, with the beetroot alongside.

minutes. Remove the pan from the heat.

Place the shallots or onions, apples and vinegar in a heavy, non-reactive frying pan and cook them over medium heat until the vinegar has evaporated and the shallots or onions are limp — about 2 minutes. Add the beef and brown it over high heat, breaking up any whole pieces as you do so. Remove the pan from the heat and stir in the thyme, some freshly ground pepper and the thickened stock.

Divide the meat mixture evenly between four small gratin dishes or place it in one large dish. Top the meat with the potato mixture, smooth the surface with a spatula, and flute the potatoes using the edge of the spatula. Brush the surface with the remaining 2 teaspoons of oil. Bake the beef and potatoes until the potatoes are lightly browned — 20 to 30 minutes.

SUGGESTED ACCOMPANIMENT: *lettuce and radish salad.*

Minced Beef with Sweet Peppers and Pasta

Serves 6
Working (and total) time: about 30 minutes

Calories **415**
Protein **28g**
Cholesterol **50mg**
Total fat **9g**
Saturated fat **3g**
Sodium **260mg**

600 g	topside of beef, trimmed of fat and minced (box, page 15)	1¼ lb
2	sweet red peppers	2
1 tbsp	olive oil	1 tbsp
2	onions, finely chopped	2
1 tsp	fennel seeds	1 tsp
6	garlic cloves, thinly sliced	6
¼ tsp	salt	¼ tsp
	freshly ground black pepper	
400 g	canned whole tomatoes, drained, seeded and chopped, the juice reserved	14 oz
6 tbsp	red wine vinegar	6 tbsp
1 tsp	sugar	1 tsp
350 g	courgettes, trimmed, halved lengthwise and cut on the diagonal into 5 mm (¼ inch) pieces	12 oz
350 g	penne or other tubular pasta	12 oz
¼ litre	unsalted chicken stock (recipe, page 138)	8 fl oz
30 g	fresh basil, shredded	1 oz
4 tbsp	freshly grated Parmesan cheese	4 tbsp

Roast the peppers about 5 cm (2 inches) below a preheated grill, turning them every now and then until their skin becomes blistered. Transfer the peppers to a bowl and cover it with plastic film; the trapped steam will loosen their skins. When the peppers are cool, peel, seed and derib them, holding them over a bowl to catch any juice. Cut the peppers into thin strips and strain the juice to remove any seeds. Set the strips and juice aside.

While the peppers are roasting, heat the oil in a heavy frying pan over medium-high heat. Add the minced beef, chopped onions, fennel seeds, sliced garlic, salt and some pepper. Cook the mixture, stirring frequently, until the beef begins to brown. Add the chopped tomatoes and their juice, the vinegar and the sugar. Reduce the heat to medium low and simmer the mixture for 10 minutes. Add the courgettes and the peppers and their juice; cook the mixture for another 5 minutes.

Meanwhile, add the pasta and ¾ teaspoon of salt to 3 litres (5 pints) of boiling water; cook the pasta for 6 minutes — it will be underdone. Drain the pasta and return it to the pan; pour in the stock, cover the pan and slowly bring the stock to a simmer. Cook the pasta for 1 minute longer, then add the beef mixture, the basil and a liberal grinding of pepper, and stir well. Simmer the mixture, stirring frequently, until most of the liquid is absorbed — 2 to 3 minutes.

Transfer the beef and pasta to a large bowl. Sprinkle the Parmesan cheese over the top and serve at once.

SUGGESTED ACCOMPANIMENT: *salad greens.*

Spicy Minced Meat on a Bed of Sweet Potatoes

Serves 4
Working time: about 1 hour
Total time: about 2 hours and 30 minutes

Calories **522**
Protein **35g**
Cholesterol **75mg**
Total fat **10g**
Saturated fat **3g**
Sodium **260mg**

600 g	topside of beef, trimmed of fat and minced (box, page 15)	1 ¼ lb
4	orange-fleshed sweet potatoes (about 1.1 kg/2 ¼ lb)	4
1.5 kg	ripe tomatoes, chopped	3 lb
2	bay leaves	2
2	cinnamon sticks	2
4	allspice berries	4
8	black peppercorns	8
2	dried red chili peppers, or ¼ tsp cayenne pepper	2
1 tbsp	tomato paste	1 tbsp
1 tsp	safflower oil	1 tsp
1	onion, finely chopped	1
¼ tsp	salt	¼ tsp
2 tbsp	chopped parsley	2 tbsp
12.5 cl	plain low-fat yogurt	4 fl oz

Preheat the oven 200°C (400°F or Mark 6). Bake the sweet potatoes for 1 hour or until they are tender when pierced with the tip of a sharp knife.

Meanwhile, put the tomatoes, bay leaves, cinnamon sticks, allspice berries, peppercorns, and chili peppers or cayenne pepper into a heavy, non-reactive pan.

Bring the mixture to the boil, then reduce the heat to medium low, and simmer it uncovered, stirring frequently, until it is reduced to ½ litre (16 fl oz) — about 1½ hours. Remove the cinnamon sticks and bay leaves from the tomato sauce, discard them, and put the sauce through a sieve. Set the sauce aside.

Sauté the beef in a large, non-stick frying pan over high heat, breaking it into chunks as it cooks. When the beef is evenly browned — about 5 minutes — add the tomato sauce and the tomato paste. Simmer the meat, partially covered to prevent splattering, until most of the liquid has evaporated — about 20 minutes. Pour the meat sauce into a bowl and keep it warm.

Peel the baked sweet potatoes and chop them coarsely. Wipe out the frying pan with a paper towel, pour in the oil and heat it over low heat. Add the onion and cook it until it is translucent — about 5 minutes. Add the sweet potatoes and 4 tablespoons of water, and cook the mixture, stirring frequently, over medium heat until the water is absorbed — about 5 minutes; stir in the salt and chopped parsley.

Place the sweet potatoes on a serving platter and top them with the meat. Serve immediately, passing the yogurt separately.

SUGGESTED ACCOMPANIMENT: *steamed mange-tout.*

Burghul-Stuffed Red Peppers

Serves 4
Working time: about 25 minutes
Total time: about 45 minutes

Calories **285**
Protein **20g**
Cholesterol **40mg**
Total fat **9g**
Saturated fat **2g**
Sodium **210mg**

350 g	topside of beef, trimmed of fat and minced (box, page 15)	12 oz
4	large sweet red or green peppers	4
1 tsp	olive oil	1 tsp
1	onion, chopped	1
2 tsp	fresh thyme, or ½ tsp dried thyme	2 tsp
125 g	mushrooms, wiped clean and thinly sliced	4 oz
2 tbsp	finely chopped celery	2 tbsp
125 g	burghul	4 oz
¼ tsp	salt	¼ tsp
	freshly ground black pepper	
35 cl	unsalted brown or chicken stock (recipes, page 138)	12 fl oz
1	garlic clove, finely chopped	1
2 tbsp	sherry vinegar or red wine vinegar	2 tbsp

Preheat the oven to 200°C (400°F or Mark 6).

To prepare the peppers, cut out and discard their stems. Slice off the peppers' tops, dice them, and set the pieces aside. Seed and derib the peppers.

Heat 1 tablespoon of the oil in a heavy saucepan over medium heat. Add half of the onion, half of the thyme, the mushrooms, celery, burghul, ⅛ teaspoon of the salt and some pepper. Cook the vegetables and burghul, stirring frequently, for 5 minutes. Add the stock, stir the mixture well, and cover the pan. Cook the mixture, stirring it occasionally, until the liquid is absorbed — about 12 minutes.

In a non-stick frying pan, heat the remaining oil over medium-high heat. When the pan is hot, add the beef, the reserved diced peppers, the remaining onion, the remaining thyme and the garlic. Cook, stirring frequently, until the beef is browned —5 to 7 minutes. Add the remaining salt, some freshly ground pepper and the vinegar. Cook the mixture for 30 seconds, then remove it from the heat.

Combine the burghul mixture with the beef and fill the peppers, mounding the filling. Bake the stuffed peppers in a shallow casserole, loosely covered with aluminium foil, for 25 minutes. Allow the peppers to stand for 5 minutes before serving them.

SUGGESTED ACCOMPANIMENT: *cucumber and onion salad.*

the lid slightly ajar, and simmer the mixture, stirring occasionally, for 1½ hours. If the tomato sauce begins to scorch, stir about 12.5 cl (4 fl oz) of water into it.

While the meat is cooking, make the coleslaw. Toss the cabbage in a bowl with the carrot, apple, yogurt, mustard, horseradish, salt and celery seeds. Cover the bowl and refrigerate it.

When the meat is done, remove it from the saucepan and let it sit at room temperature. Add the celery leaves, lemon juice, brown sugar, Tabasco sauce, salt and some pepper to the tomato mixture. Coarsely chop the beef and add it also. Simmer the barbecue beef over low heat for 30 minutes.

Split the rolls and fill them with the beef, topped with some of the coleslaw.

Beef Barbecue Sandwiches

Serves 8
Working time: about 45 minutes
Total time: about 2 hours and 30 minutes

Calories **380**
Protein **34g**
Cholesterol **85mg**
Total fat **10g**
Saturated fat **3g**
Sodium **435mg**

1.25 g	rolled topside of beef or top rump, trimmed of fat	2½ lb
800 g	canned whole tomatoes, puréed in a food processor or a blender, and sieved	1¾ lb
1	onion, finely chopped	1
17.5 cl	cider vinegar	6 fl oz
30 g	celery leaves, finely chopped	1 oz
1	lemon, juice only	1
4 tbsp	light brown sugar	4 tbsp
10	drops Tabasco sauce	10
¼ tsp	salt	¼ tsp
	freshly ground black pepper	
8	large soft bread rolls	8
Coleslaw		
300 g	white cabbage, shredded	10 oz
1	small carrot, grated	1
1	red apple, grated	1
¼ litre	plain low-fat yogurt	8 fl oz
½ tsp	dry mustard	½ tsp
1 tsp	prepared horseradish	1 tsp
¼ tsp	salt	¼ tsp
½ tsp	celery seeds	½ tsp

Pour the puréed tomatoes into a large saucepan along with ¾ litre (1¼ pints) of water. Add the onion, vinegar and beef, and bring the liquid to a simmer over medium heat. Reduce the heat, cover the pan, leaving

Spicy Minced Beef Baked in Corn Bread

Serves 4
Working time: about 25 minutes
Total time: about 1 hour

Calories **395**
Protein **28g**
Cholesterol **55mg**
Total fat **10g**
Saturated fat **3g**
Sodium **325mg**

500 g	topside of beef, trimmed of fat, minced (box, page 15), and crumbled into small pieces	1 lb
1	onion, chopped	1
½	sweet green pepper, seeded, deribbed and diced	½
3	garlic cloves, thinly sliced	3
1 tsp	chili powder	1 tsp
1 tsp	dry mustard	1 tsp
¼ tsp	cayenne pepper	¼ tsp
400 g	canned whole tomatoes, drained	14 oz
1 tsp	sugar	1 tsp
6 tbsp	red wine vinegar	6 tbsp
⅛ tsp	salt	⅛ tsp
Corn bread		
80 g	cornmeal	2¾ oz
90 g	plain flour	3 oz
1 tbsp	sugar	1 tbsp
1½ tsp	baking powder	1½ tsp
½ tsp	chili powder	½ tsp
1 tbsp	safflower oil	1 tbsp
17.5 cl	semi-skimmed milk	6 fl oz
1	egg white	1

Heat a large, non-stick frying pan over medium-high heat. Combine the beef, onion, green pepper, garlic, chili powder, mustard and cayenne pepper in the pan. Stir the mixture frequently, until the beef is cooked through — 4 to 5 minutes. Add the tomatoes, sugar, vinegar and salt, crushing the tomatoes; cook the mixture until most of the liquid has evaporated — 15 to 20 minutes. Set it aside.

Preheat the oven to 230°C (450°F or Mark 8).

To make the corn bread, sift the cornmeal, flour, sugar, baking powder and chili powder into a bowl. Add the oil, stir well, and work the oil into the dry ingredients with your fingertips until no lumps remain; the mixture will be very dry. In a separate bowl, whisk the milk and the egg white together, and add the liquid to the cornmeal mixture. Stir gently just to incor-porate the liquid; do not overmix.

Lightly oil a 1.5 litre (2½ pint) baking dish. Pour the corn-bread batter into the dish. Spoon the beef and vegetables into the centre of the batter, leaving a 3.5 cm (1½ inch) border all round. Bake the mixture for 25 minutes. Remove the dish from the oven and let it stand for 5 minutes before serving.

SUGGESTED ACCOMPANIMENT: *sweet red pepper and spring onion salad.*

Suetcrust Steak and Chestnut Pie

THE VEGETARIAN SUET USED TO MAKE THE CRUST FOR THIS PIE IS
AVAILABLE FROM HEALTH FOOD SHOPS AND LARGE SUPERMARKETS.
IT DOES NOT CONTAIN SATURATED FAT AND IS THEREFORE A
HEALTHY ALTERNATIVE TO BEEF SUET.

Serves 6
Working time: about 45 minutes
Total time: about 2 hours and 45 minutes (includes cooling)

Calories **300**
Protein **21g**
Cholesterol **45mg**
Total fat **20g**
Saturated fat **5g**
Sodium **140mg**

500 g	rump steak, trimmed of fat and cut into 2.5 cm (1 inch) cubes	1 lb
1	onion, sliced	1
8 cl	fresh orange juice	3 fl oz
12.5 cl	brown stock (page 138)	4 fl oz
½	orange, grated rind only	½
125 g	peeled fresh chestnuts, or dried chestnuts, soaked overnight	4 oz
1 tbsp	tomato paste	1 tbsp
1 tsp	chopped fresh thyme, or ¼ tsp dried thyme	1 tsp
	freshly ground black pepper	
⅛ tsp	salt	⅛ tsp
6	carrots, sliced	6
4	sticks celery, cut diagonally into 2.5 cm (1 inch) slices	4
250 g	button mushrooms, wiped	8 oz
1 to 2 tbsp	skimmed milk, to glaze	1 to 2 tbsp
Suetcrust		
175 g	plain flour	6 oz
1½ tsp	baking powder	1½ tsp
½ tsp	dry mustard	½ tsp
⅛ tsp	salt	⅛ tsp
90 g	vegetarian suet, or hard white vegetable fat, well chilled	3 oz

Put the steak and sliced onion in a heavy fireproof casserole and add the orange juice and stock. Bring to the boil, then add the orange rind, chestnuts, tomato paste, thyme, pepper and salt. Reduce the heat, cover and simmer for 30 minutes. Add the carrots and celery and simmer for a further 30 minutes. Remove from the heat, stir in the mushrooms and turn into a 90 cl (1½ pint) pie dish. Leave to cool.

To make the suetcrust, preheat the oven to 200°C

(400°F or Mark 6). Sift the flour, baking powder, mustard and salt into a bowl. Coarsely grate the vegetable fat and add to the flour. With a palette knife, mix in 12.5 to 15 cl (4 to 5 fl oz) of cold water to make a soft but not sticky dough. Knead lightly until just smooth.

Roll out the pastry on a floured surface until it is 2.5 cm (1 inch) larger than the top of the pie dish. Cut 1 cm (½ inch) wide strips from the edge of the pastry and press on to the dampened rim of the pie dish. Dampen the pastry rim and lift the large piece of pastry on top of

the pie. Press together to seal, trim the edge and crimp it. Make a hole in the centre.

Brush the pastry with skimmed milk, then decorate with pastry trimmings and brush these also with the milk. Place the pie dish on a baking sheet and bake for 45 minutes or until the pastry is golden-brown. Serve hot, straight from the dish.

SUGGESTED ACCOMPANIMENT: *a green vegetable such as broccoli, Brussels sprouts or spring cabbage.*

Bobotie

Serves 8
Working time: about 40 minutes
Total time: about 2 hours

Calories **270**
Protein **28g**
Cholesterol **100mg**
Total fat **10g**
Saturated fat **3g**
Sodium **260mg**

700 g	topside of beef, trimmed of fat and minced (page 15)	1½ lb
5 tsp	safflower oil	5 tsp
2	onions, chopped	2
1	garlic clove, crushed	1
2 tsp	turmeric	2 tsp
2 tsp	ground cumin	2 tsp
2 tsp	ground coriander	2 tsp
1 tsp	chili powder	1 tsp
1 tsp	ground cinnamon	1 tsp
1 tsp	ground ginger	1 tsp
½ tsp	salt	½ tsp
	freshly ground black pepper	
60 g	sultanas	2 oz
60 g	raisins	2 oz
4 tbsp	cider vinegar	4 tbsp
125 g	fresh wholemeal breadcrumbs	4 oz
15 cl	skimmed milk	¼ pint
15 cl	plain low-fat yogurt	¼ pint
2	eggs, beaten	2
30 g	flaked almonds	1 oz
4 to 6	small bay leaves	4 to 6

Heat 4 teaspoons of the oil in a small non-stick frying pan over medium heat. Cook the onion and garlic in the oil until softened — about 5 minutes. Add the tur- ▶

meric, cumin, coriander, chili powder, cinnamon, ginger, salt and some pepper, and cook, stirring, for 30 seconds. Tip the spiced mixture into a mixing bowl. Add the minced beef, sultanas, raisins and vinegar.

Preheat the oven to 180°C (350°F or Mark 4). Put the breadcrumbs and milk in a small bowl, and stir together with a fork. Drain the crumbs in a sieve over a bowl and reserve the milk, pressing the crumbs to extract all excess liquid. Add the breadcrumbs to the beef mixture and work together with your hands until thoroughly amalgamated.

Use the remaining teaspoon of oil to grease a deep 3 litre (5 pint) ovenproof dish. Pack the beef mixture into the dish and smooth the surface.

Mix the reserved milk with the yogurt and beaten eggs and pour over the meat mixture. Scatter the almonds over the top and decorate with the bay leaves. Bake for 1¼ hours, or until the topping is set and golden-brown. Serve hot.

SUGGESTED ACCOMPANIMENT: *oakleaf lettuce and curly endive salad.*

Veal, Peach and Peppercorn Pâté

Serves 8
Working time: about 30 minutes
Total time: 1½ to 2 days (includes marinating and chilling)

Calories **250**
Protein **13g**
Cholesterol **75mg**
Total fat **4g**
Saturated fat **2g**
Sodium **200mg**

500 g	topside of veal, trimmed of fat and cut into 2.5 cm (1 inch) dice	1 lb
125 g	dried peaches, diced	4 oz
12.5 cl	dry white wine	4 fl oz
30	fresh green peppercorns, 10 crushed	30
125 g	fresh brown breadcrumbs	4 oz
1	lemon, finely grated rind and juice	1
2 tbsp	brandy	2 tbsp
1	egg, beaten	1
¼ tsp	ground allspice	¼ tsp
⅛ tsp	salt	⅛ tsp
	fresh green peppercorn sprigs for garnish (optional)	
	Peach sauce	
60 g	dried peaches	2 oz
8 cl	dry white wine	3 fl oz
⅛ tsp	ground allspice	⅛ tsp

Place the diced veal, peaches and wine in a bowl, cover and leave to marinate in a cold place or the refrigerator for 24 hours, turning occasionally.

Preheat the oven to 170°C (325°F or Mark 3). Put the veal, peaches and any remaining liquid in a food processor, chop finely, then transfer the mixture to a large bowl. Add the whole and crushed peppercorns, bread-crumbs, grated lemon rind and juice, brandy, egg, allspice and salt. Mix thoroughly.

Line the bottom of a 1 kg (2 lb) loaf tin with dampened greaseproof paper. Pack the pâté mixture into the tin and smooth the surface. Cover with foil, stand the tin in a roasting pan and pour in enough boiling water to come half way up the sides of the tin. Cook in the oven for 1 hour. Remove the tin from the water and leave the pâté to cool.

When cool, take off the foil, cover the surface of the pâté with dampened greaseproof paper and weight it down with a weighted board. Chill in the refrigerator for 8 hours or overnight.

To make the peach sauce, put the dried peaches in a heavy-bottomed saucepan, add ½ litre (16 fl oz) of water and the wine, and bring to the boil. Reduce the heat, cover and simmer very gently until the peaches are tender — about 30 minutes. Transfer the peaches and their cooking liquid to a food processor and blend until smooth. Pour the purée into a jug, add 15 cl (¼ pint) of water and the allspice, and whisk vigorously. Leave the sauce to cool, then chill it in the refrigerator until serving time.

To serve, turn the pâté out of the tin and cut it into 16 thin slices. Arrange two slices on individual plates and garnish with peppercorn sprigs, if using. Whisk the sauce, adding, if necessary, a few spoonfuls of water or wine to thin it down. Spoon a little sauce on each plate and pass the remainder separately.

SUGGESTED ACCOMPANIMENT: *grated celeriac tossed in a little mayonnaise and lemon juice.*

Hot Veal and Spinach Terrine

Serves 8 as a starter, 4 as a main course
Working time: about 30 minutes
Total time: about 1 hour and 40 minutes

Calories **130**
Protein **16g**
Cholesterol **80mg**
Total fat **6g**
Saturated fat **2g**
Sodium **260mg**

500 g	topside of veal, trimmed of fat and diced	1 lb
350 g	fresh young spinach leaves, coarse stems removed, washed	12 oz
¼ tsp	freshly grated nutmeg	¼ tsp
¼ tsp	salt	¼ tsp
8 tbsp	low-fat soft cheese, such as quark	8 tbsp
2 tbsp	whipping cream	2 tbsp
1	egg	1
20	juniper berries, crushed	20
2 tbsp	dry sherry	2 tbsp
	freshly ground black pepper	
2	egg whites	2
15 cl	buttermilk	¼ pint
1 tsp	light grainy mustard	1 tsp

Blanch the spinach in a large saucepan of boiling water for 10 seconds only. Drain the leaves, rinse them under cold running water and dry them carefully with a clean tea towel. Use enough spinach leaves to line the base and sides of a 1 litre (1¾ pint) terrine, letting them overhang the edges. Put the remaining leaves in a food processor together with the nutmeg and half the salt, and chop finely. Transfer the spinach to a bowl and set aside to cool.

Preheat the oven to 180°C (350°F or Mark 4). Mince the veal in the food processor, add the cheese, cream, whole egg, crushed juniper berries, sherry, some freshly ground pepper and the remaining salt, and process until all the ingredients are evenly mixed. Transfer the mixture to a bowl.

Whisk the egg whites until stiff, then fold them into the veal. Spoon half the mixture into the terrine and smooth the surface. Spoon the chopped spinach in a layer on top, then cover with the remaining veal and again smooth the surface. Cover with the overhanging spinach leaves, then with foil. Stand the terrine in a roasting pan, pour in enough boiling water to come half way up the sides of the terrine and cook in the oven for 1 hour.

Meanwhile, whisk the buttermilk and mustard together in a jug. Remove the terrine from the water, take off the foil, pour off any excess liquid and leave to stand for 5 minutes. Run a knife round the edge of the terrine and turn it out on to a board. Carve it into neat slices and arrange them on individual plates. Pour some of the buttermilk sauce over each portion.

EDITOR'S NOTE: *This dish can also be served cold — in which case leave it to cool in the terrine before turning out.*

Fricadelles with Cucumber Sauce

THESE DILL-FLAVOURED MEAT PATTIES ARE A VERSION OF DANISH FRIKADELLER, WHICH ARE TRADITIONALLY TORPEDO-SHAPED.

Serves 6
Working (and total) time: about 1 hour

Calories **165**
Protein **16g**
Cholesterol **70mg**
Total fat **6g**
Saturated fat **2g**
Sodium **205mg**

600 g	topside of veal, trimmed of fat and diced	1 ¼ lb
2	slices wholemeal bread, crusts removed	2
1	onion, grated	1
3 tbsp	sparkling mineral water	3 tbsp
2	egg whites	2
1 tsp	chopped fresh dill	1 tsp
½ tsp	ground allspice	½ tsp
⅛ tsp	salt	⅛ tsp
	freshly ground black pepper	
1 tbsp	virgin olive oil	1 tbsp
Cucumber sauce		
1	large cucumber, peeled and finely diced	1
15 cl	unsalted chicken or veal stock (recipes, page 138)	¼ pint
4 tbsp	Greek-style strained yogurt	4 tbsp
2 tsp	cornflour	2 tsp
1 ½ tsp	chopped fresh dill	1 ½ tsp
⅛ tsp	salt	⅛ tsp
	white pepper	

Put the veal in a food processor with the bread, onion, mineral water, egg whites, dill, allspice, salt and some pepper, and mince finely. Transfer the mixture to a bowl. Dip two dessert spoons into hot water and use to form the minced mixture into about 30 torpedo shapes, dipping the spoons back into the hot water after forming each one.

Heat the oil in a large, non-stick sauté or frying pan over medium heat. Add the fricadelles and cook until browned on all sides — about 10 minutes — gently turning once. Transfer the patties to a warmed dish, cover and keep hot while preparing the sauce.

Add the cucumber to the pan and stir-fry for 1 minute. Pour in the stock, bring to the boil and simmer for 2 to 3 minutes. Mix the yogurt and cornflour together, add a few spoonfuls of the hot stock, then add to the pan and whisk over gentle heat for 2 minutes. Add the dill, the salt and some white pepper. Serve hot, passing the sauce separately.

SUGGESTED ACCOMPANIMENT: *beetroot and lettuce salad.*

Veal and Pasta Loaf with Tomato-Basil Ketchup

Serves 12 as a starter
Working time: about 1 hour and 10 minutes
Total time: about 2 hours and 20 minutes

Calories **143**
Protein **6g**
Cholesterol **55mg**
Total fat **3g**
Saturated fat **1g**
Sodium **115mg**

500 g	topside of veal or top rump, trimmed of fat and minced (page 15)	1 lb
1 tsp	olive oil	1 tsp
1	onion, chopped	1
1	small garlic clove, crushed	1
150 g	courgettes, trimmed and grated	5 oz
150 g	carrot, grated	5 oz
150 g	parsnip, grated	5 oz
½ tsp	salt	½ tsp
	freshly ground black pepper	
1	egg	1
1	egg white	1
250 g	rigatoni or other small pasta shapes	8 oz
1 tbsp	cornflour	1 tbsp
15 cl	semi-skimmed milk	¼ pint
¼ tsp	grated nutmeg	¼ tsp
1 tbsp	freshly grated Parmesan cheese	1 tbsp

Tomato-basil ketchup

750 g	ripe tomatoes, skinned, seeded and chopped, or 400g (14 oz) canned tomatoes, chopped	1½ lb
1 tsp	tomato paste	1 tsp
½ tsp	caster sugar	½ tsp
6	fresh basil leaves, shredded	6

Heat the oil in a small, non-stick frying pan over medium heat. Add the onion, garlic and 2 tablespoons of water and cook for about 5 minutes or until softened, stirring occasionally. Tip the onion and garlic into a mixing bowl and add the veal, courgettes, carrot, parsnip, half the salt and some pepper.

Lightly beat the egg and egg white together in a small bowl. Add half the egg to the veal mixture and work together thoroughly with your hands. Set aside. Cook the rigatoni in 3 litres (5 pints) of boiling water with 1½ teaspoons of salt. Start testing the pasta after 10 minutes and cook until it is *al dente*.

Meanwhile, make the white sauce. Mix the cornflour with a little of the milk in a small cup. Put the remaining milk in a small saucepan and bring to the boil, then reduce the heat. Add the cornflour mixture, stirring vigorously, and simmer gently for 3 minutes, stirring constantly. Remove from the heat and cool slightly, then stir in the remaining egg mixture, the remaining salt and the nutmeg. Drain the pasta, put it back in the pan and mix with the white sauce.

Preheat the oven to 170°C (325°F or Mark 3). Line the bottom of a 1 kg (2 lb) loaf tin with a piece of dampened greaseproof paper. Make a layer of just under one third of the meat mixture on the bottom of the tin, pressing and spreading it out evenly. Cover with half the pasta, then make another layer of the meat mixture. Top with the remaining pasta and finish

with the rest of the meat mixture. (When laying the meat mixture over the pasta, press the mixture between your hands first, cover a small area at a time and smooth over with the back of a spoon.) Sprinkle the top of the layered loaf with the Parmesan cheese. Place the tin in a roasting pan and pour in enough boiling water to come at least 2.5 cm (1 inch) up the sides of the tin. Bake for 1 hour.

Meanwhile, make the tomato-basil ketchup. Put the tomatoes into a small, heavy-bottomed saucepan,

adding a little water if using fresh tomatoes, and simmer until well reduced — about 10 minutes — stirring from time to time. Sieve the tomatoes and mix in the tomato paste and sugar. Allow to cool.

When the loaf is ready, let it cool in the tin for 10 minutes before turning it out. Remove the lining paper, then turn over on to a cutting board. Cut into thick slices. Stir the basil into the ketchup and serve with the loaf.

Veal and Mushroom Burgers with Mango-Pineapple Relish

Serves 4
Working time: about 50 minutes
Total time: about 1 hour and 35 minutes

Calories **325**
Protein **22g**
Cholesterol **70mg**
Total fat **9g**
Saturated fat **3g**
Sodium **370mg**

350 g	topside of veal or top rump, trimmed of fat and finely chopped (page 15)	12 oz
175 g	chestnut or button mushrooms, stems wiped clean and finely chopped	6 oz
30 g	shelled walnuts, finely chopped	1 oz
½ tsp	salt	½ tsp
	freshly ground black pepper	
⅛ to ¼ tsp	cayenne pepper	⅛ to ¼ tsp
1	egg white	1
2	wholemeal muffins, split in half	2
	watercress or shredded lettuce	
	Mango-pineapple relish	
1	small unripe mango (about 250 g/8 oz), peeled, stoned and finely diced	1
250 g	fresh pineapple, finely diced	8 oz
1	small onion, finely chopped	1
1½ tsp	freshly grated ginger root	1½ tsp
1	small cinnamon stick	1
4	cloves	4
1	bay leaf	1
1	lime, grated rind and juice	1
½ tsp	Chinese chili sauce	½ tsp

To make the relish, put the diced mango and pineapple into a heavy-bottomed saucepan and add the onion, ginger, cinnamon, cloves, bay leaf, and lime rind and juice. Cover and cook gently for about 45 minutes, stirring occasionally, until the fruit is very tender. Add a tablespoon of water from time to time to prevent the relish sticking to the pan. When cooked, remove and discard the cinnamon stick, cloves and bay leaf. Stir in the chili sauce and allow to cool.

To make the burgers, put the veal, mushrooms and

walnuts in a bowl, add the salt, some pepper and the cayenne pepper, and work the mixture with your hands, adding enough egg white to bind. Divide the mixture into four portions and shape each into a neat burger about 1 cm (½ inch) thick. Place the burgers on a plate, cover and chill for 20 minutes.

Preheat the grill. Grill the burgers for 8 to 10 minutes on each side or until cooked through and golden-brown, turning them over carefully to avoid breaking them. Just before the burgers have finished cooking, toast the muffins on both sides. Cover the muffin halves with watercress or shredded lettuce and place a burger on top. Serve immediately with the relish.

SUGGESTED ACCOMPANIMENT: *cabbage and carrot coleslaw.*

EDITOR'S NOTE: *Alternatively, the meat, mushrooms and walnuts can be finely chopped in a food processor, but the mixture will have a much smoother texture.*

5 *Green peppercorns, garlic and parsley enliven a beef roast that was braised on a bed of mushrooms and onions in the microwave oven (recipe, opposite).*

Microwaving Beef and Veal

A microwave oven encourages invention — and never more so, perhaps, than in the case of beef and veal, for the meat may be prepared successfully in any number of ways in a fraction of the time it would take by conventional cooking methods. Sealed in an oven-cooking bag and microwaved on medium power, for example, a roast braises in its own juices. It might also be cut into strips for a dish that looks and tastes like a stir-fry with very little oil, or stuffed with a vegetable filling and served sliced.

Particular success attends recipes based on minced meat. The veal meatballs on page 137 are served with a red and green pepper sauce, while a Latin American *picadillo (recipe, page 128)* highlights minced beef combined with raisins and olives.

A few simple techniques ensure success. Cutting beef or veal into smaller pieces helps it cook more evenly in the microwave oven, but roasts can also be cooked whole. To keep the meat from drying out, cover the roast during cooking. Avoid salting the roast beforehand — this tends to toughen the meat and leach natural salts and moisture.

For the sake of succulence, tender cuts of beef and veal — including escalopes and meatballs — should be microwaved on high (100 per cent power). Less tender cuts, such as those from topside of beef, should be tightly covered and then simmered in liquid on medium (50 per cent power).

Because food continues to cook after it emerges from the microwave oven, achieving the desired degree of doneness involves "standing time". Remove a roast from the oven slightly before the meat looks cooked, then insert an instant-reading thermometer in the centre and let the meat stand until it reaches the proper internal temperature. In general, the standing time equals one third to one half of the cooking time; where such a step is required, the recipe instructions specify how long.

Many of the recipes on the following pages use a browning dish. This dish, designed specifically for the microwave oven, has a special coating on its base which enables the meat to be seared and browned in much the same way as under a grill or in a frying pan. When using a microwave browning dish it is important to follow the manufacturer's instructions carefully, as overheating can cause damage.

Beef Braised on Mushrooms with Green Peppercorn Persillade

Serves 6
Working time: about 30 minutes
Total time: about 1 hour

Calories **200**
Protein **25g**
Cholesterol **60mg**
Total fat **7g**
Saturated fat **2g**
Sodium **140mg**

850 g	boned and rolled sirloin joint, trimmed of fat	1¾ lb
500 g	mushrooms, wiped clean and thinly sliced	1 lb
1	onion, finely chopped	1
1 tsp	safflower oil	1 tsp
2 tsp	green peppercorns, rinsed	2 tsp
30 g	parsley leaves	1 oz
3	garlic cloves	3
¼ tsp	salt	¼ tsp
2 tbsp	plain flour	2 tbsp

Combine the mushrooms, onion and oil in a 20 cm (8 inch) square baking dish. Cover the dish with plastic film and microwave the vegetables on high for 5 minutes.

While the mushrooms are cooking, prepare the green peppercorn persillade. Place the green peppercorns, parsley and garlic on a chopping board and sprinkle them with the salt; finely chop the mixture.

Pierce the roast in about 15 places with the tip of a small knife. Press some of the persillade into each of the incisions. Rub away any remaining persillade on the outside of the roast.

When the mushrooms have finished cooking, stir the flour into them. Set the roast on top of the mushrooms and cover the dish once again. Cook the meat on medium (50 per cent power) for 14 to 16 minutes for medium-rare meat. Let the roast stand, still covered, an additional 10 minutes before carving. (At this point, the internal temperature of the meat should have risen to 63°C (145°F); if it has not, microwave the roast on high for 2 to 3 minutes more.)

Cut the roast into very thin slices; divide the meat and mushrooms between six warmed dinner plates. Serve immediately.

SUGGESTED ACCOMPANIMENT: *steamed potatoes and carrots.*

Picadillo

THIS ADAPTATION OF A LATIN AMERICAN FAVOURITE
FEATURES SULTANAS, OLIVES AND CHICK-PEAS IN ADDITION
TO THE CHOPPED MEAT

Serves 6
Working time: about 45 minutes
Total time: about 3 hours (includes soaking)

Calories **225**
Protein **18g**
Cholesterol **35mg**
Total fat **6g**
Saturated fat **1g**
Sodium **235mg**

500 g	topside of beef, trimmed of fat and minced (box, page 15)	1 lb
200 g	dried chick-peas, picked over	7 oz
1	onion, chopped	1
4	garlic cloves, finely chopped	4
1 tsp	safflower oil	1 tsp
800 g	canned whole tomatoes, drained and crushed	1¾ lb
75 g	sultanas	2½ oz
12	green olives, stoned and rinsed	12
½ tsp	ground cinnamon	½ tsp
½ tsp	ground allspice	½ tsp
¼ tsp	cayenne pepper	¼ tsp
2	bay leaves	2

Rinse the chick-peas under cold running water, then put them into a large, heavy saucepan with enough water to cover them by about 7.5 cm (3 inches). Cover the pan, leaving the lid ajar, and slowly bring the liquid to the boil over medium-low heat. Boil the chick-peas for 2 minutes, then turn off the heat, and soak the chick-peas, covered, for at least 1 hour. Return the chick-peas to the boil, reduce the heat, and simmer them until they are tender — about 1 hour.

Combine the chopped onion, garlic and safflower oil in a large bowl, cover the bowl with plastic film and microwave the vegetables on high for 4 minutes. Add the minced beef and cook the mixture, uncovered, on medium (50 per cent power) for 5 minutes. Stir the beef, breaking it into small pieces, and cook it on medium for 3 minutes more.

Drain the chick-peas and add them to the beef mixture. Stir in the tomatoes, sultanas, olives, cinnamon, allspice, cayenne pepper and bay leaves. Cook the picadillo, uncovered, on high for 15 minutes, stirring it every 5 minutes. Remove the bay leaves and let the picadillo stand for 5 minutes before serving.

SUGGESTED ACCOMPANIMENT: *rice with sweet red pepper.*

EDITOR'S NOTE: *Canned chick-peas can be used in this recipe, thus greatly reducing the cooking time, but the sodium content of the dish will be increased.*

Meatballs in Caper Sauce

Serves 4 as an appetizer
Working time: about 20 minutes
Total time: about 30 minutes

Calories **120**
Protein **14g**
Cholesterol **35mg**
Total fat **4g**
Saturated fat **1g**
Sodium **190mg**

300 g	topside of beef, trimmed of fat and minced (box, page 15)	10 oz
1	small onion, chopped	1
¼ litre	unsalted brown or chicken stock (recipes, page 138)	8 fl oz
4 tbsp	rolled oats	4 tbsp
1 tbsp	chopped parsley	1 tbsp
¼ tsp	grated nutmeg	¼ tsp
1	lemon, grated rind only	1
	freshly ground black pepper	
1 tsp	cornflour, mixed with 1 tbsp water	1 tsp
1 tbsp	plain low-fat yogurt	1 tbsp
1 tsp	soured cream	1 tsp
1 tsp	capers, rinsed and chopped	1 tsp

Put the onion in a 1 litre (1¾ pint) baking dish. Cover the dish and microwave the onion on high for 3 minutes. Transfer the onion to a bowl. Pour the stock into the baking dish and cook it on high until it comes to a simmer — about 4 minutes.

While the stock is heating, add the beef, rolled oats, ½ tablespoon of the parsley, the nutmeg, the lemon rind and a liberal grinding of pepper to the onion. Knead the mixture to mix it well, then form it into 16 meatballs. Drop the meatballs into the heated stock and cook them, covered, on high for 4 minutes.

Using a slotted spoon, transfer the meatballs to a serving dish. Discard all but 12.5 cl (4 fl oz) of the cooking liquid in the baking dish; stir the cornflour mixture into this remaining liquid. Cook the liquid on high until it thickens — about 30 seconds. Turn off the heat and let the thickened stock cool for 1 minute, then stir in the yogurt, soured cream, capers and the remaining parsley. Pour the sauce over the meatballs and serve them while they are still hot.

Lime-Ginger Beef

Serves 4
Working time: about 25 minutes
Total time: about 45 minutes

Calories **240**
Protein **25g**
Cholesterol **65mg**
Total fat **10g**
Saturated fat **3g**
Sodium **180mg**

600 g	rump steak, trimmed of fat and cut into thin strips	1¼ lb
	freshly ground black pepper	
1 tbsp	safflower oil	1 tbsp
2	spring onions, trimmed and sliced into thin strips	2
1	large carrot, julienned	1
1	sweet red pepper, seeded, deribbed and julienned	1
Lime-ginger sauce		
1	lime, grated rind and juice	1
1 tsp	grated fresh ginger root	1 tsp
2 tbsp	dry sherry	2 tbsp
2 tsp	low-sodium soy sauce or shoyu	2 tsp
½ tsp	finely chopped garlic	½ tsp
1 tbsp	sugar	1 tbsp
1 tbsp	cornflour, mixed with 4 tbsp water	1 tbsp

Preheat a microwave browning dish on high for the maximum time allowed in the dish's instruction manual. While the dish is heating, combine all the ingredients for the lime-ginger sauce in a small bowl. Set the bowl aside. Season the beef strips with a generous grinding of black pepper.

When the browning dish is heated, brush ½ tablespoon of the oil evenly over the dish to coat it. Sear half of the beef strips on the dish, stirring and turning the meat with a wooden spoon. Once the beef has been seared — after 1 or 2 minutes — transfer it to a baking dish. Wipe off the browning dish with a paper towel and reheat it for 3 minutes. Brush the remaining oil on to the dish and sear the remaining beef in the same way. Add the beef to the baking dish.

Add the spring onions, carrot and red pepper to the beef. Pour the sauce over all and microwave the mixture on high for 3 minutes. Serve the beef and vegetables from the baking dish or transfer them to a platter; serve at once.

SUGGESTED ACCOMPANIMENT: *steamed rice.*

Escalopes in Tarragon and Mushroom Sauce

Serves 4
Working time: about 15 minutes
Total time: about 1 hour and 15 minutes (includes marinating)

Calories **240**
Protein **22g**
Cholesterol **100mg**
Total fat **11g**
Saturated fat **3g**
Sodium **215mg**

4	thin veal escalopes (about 125 g/4 oz each)	4
2 tbsp	virgin olive oil	2 tbsp
2 tbsp	finely shredded fresh tarragon leaves	2 tbsp
	freshly ground black pepper	
Mushroom sauce		
175 g	mushrooms, trimmed and very thinly sliced	6 oz
4 tbsp	Marsala	4 tbsp
15 g	plain flour	½ oz
2 tbsp	soured cream mixed with enough skimmed milk to make 15 cl (¼ pint)	2 tbsp
¼ tsp	salt	¼ tsp

Blend the oil with 1 tablespoon of the tarragon and some pepper in a shallow dish. Add the escalopes and turn them in the oil until they are evenly coated. Cover the dish and leave to marinate at room temperature for at least 1 hour.

Heat a browning dish on high for the maximum time allowed in the instruction manual. Brown the escalopes on each side in the hot dish, then cover and microwave on high for 1½ minutes. Transfer the escalopes to a plate, cover and set aside.

To make the sauce, stir the Marsala into the browning dish, add the mushrooms and microwave on high for 2 minutes. Blend the flour with the soured cream mixture, remaining tarragon, salt and a little black pepper until smooth. Stir into the mushrooms and microwave on high for 1 minute. Return the escalopes to the dish, coat well with the sauce and microwave for 2½ to 3 minutes, repositioning the escalopes half way through cooking. Serve immediately.

SUGGESTED ACCOMPANIMENTS: *savoury rice with peas, spring onions and sweet peppers; French bread.*

Microwave Stir-Fry

Serves 4
Working (and total) time: about 25 minutes

Calories **260**
Protein **24g**
Cholesterol **90mg**
Total fat **14g**
Saturated fat **3g**
Sodium **140mg**

500 g	thin veal escalopes, cut into very thin strips	1 lb
250 g	broccoli, trimmed and cut into small florets	8 oz
2 tbsp	virgin olive oil	2 tbsp
3 tbsp	hoisin sauce	3 tbsp
1	small sweet red pepper, cut into thin julienne	1
125 g	radishes, thinly sliced	4 oz
1	garlic clove, crushed	1
175 g	fresh pineapple flesh, cut into small pieces	6 oz
30 g	unsalted cashew nuts	1 oz

Put the broccoli into a dish with 2 tablespoons of water, cover and microwave on high for 1½ minutes. Pour into a colander and rinse under cold water to refresh. Drain well and set aside.

Heat a browning dish on high for the maximum time allowed in the instruction manual. Add 1 tablespoon of the oil and the veal strips. Microwave on high for 1½ minutes, stirring once. Remove the veal from the dish and set aside.

Mix 1 tablespoon of the meat juices from the browning dish with the hoisin sauce and pour the rest away. Add the remaining oil to the browning dish and microwave on high for 30 seconds. Add the julienned red pepper, sliced radishes and crushed garlic, and microwave on high for 1 minute.

Stir in the pineapple, cashew nuts and broccoli florets, then microwave on high for 1 minute. Add the veal and hoisin sauce, stir well and microwave on high for 2½ to 3 minutes, stirring half way through cooking. Serve immediately.

SUGGESTED ACCOMPANIMENT: *steamed rice.*

Courgette-Stuffed Veal Rump

Serves 4
Working time: about 40 minutes
Total time: about 1 hour and 50 minutes (includes marinating)

Calories **240**
Protein **22g**
Cholesterol **90mg**
Total fat **13g**
Saturated fat **3g**
Sodium **210mg**

500 g	veal rump in one piece, trimmed of fat	1 lb
1 tbsp	virgin olive oil	1 tbsp
1	garlic clove, crushed	1
1 tsp	paprika	1 tsp
2 tbsp	brandy	2 tbsp
Courgette stuffing		
1 tbsp	virgin olive oil	1 tbsp
1	small onion, very finely chopped	1
350 g	courgettes, coarsely grated	12 oz
1 tbsp	chopped fresh marjoram, or 1 tsp dried marjoram	1 tbsp
¼ tsp	salt	¼ tsp
	freshly ground black pepper	
30 g	black olives, stoned and finely chopped	1 oz

Slice the veal horizontally almost in two *(Step 1, box, opposite)*. Open it out flat and place between two sheets of plastic film, then beat with a meat bat, as illustrated in Step 1 on page 32. Put in the refrigerator while making the stuffing.

Place the oil in a shallow dish, add the onion and microwave on high for 2 minutes until softened. Stir in the courgettes, cover and microwave on high for 7 to 8 minutes until they are softened, stirring every 2 minutes. Remove from the microwave, stir in the marjoram, salt, some pepper and the olives. Allow to cool.

Spread the stuffing evenly over one half of the flattened veal, then fold the other half over to enclose the stuffing and tie securely *(Steps 2 and 3, opposite)*.

Blend the olive oil, garlic and paprika together in a shallow dish, add the veal and turn it gently in this marinade until it is evenly coated. Cover and marinate at room temperature for 1 hour.

Heat a browning dish on high for the maximum time allowed in the instruction manual. Transfer the veal to the browning dish and brown on both sides. Cover and microwave on high for 5 minutes, turning it over after 2½ minutes. Transfer the veal to a serving plate, cover with foil and allow to stand for 2 minutes, then carefully remove the string. Meanwhile, stir the brandy into the dish, microwave on high for 2 minutes and strain over the veal. Serve the veal hot or cold, cut into thin slices.

SUGGESTED ACCOMPANIMENT: *mange-tout.*

Stuffing and Trussing a Veal Rump

1 MAKING A POCKET. With a sharp knife, slice the veal (here a piece of rump) horizontally almost in two. Lay the veal on a sheet of plastic film. Open out the meat and cover it with a second piece of plastic.

2 SPREADING THE STUFFING. Using a meat bat, gently pound the meat until it spreads enough to accommodate a stuffing. Spoon the stuffing (recipe, opposite) evenly over one half of the flattened veal. Fold the other half of the veal over to enclose the stuffing.

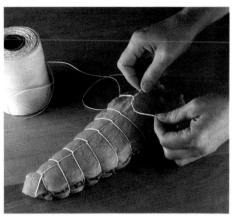

3 SECURING THE STUFFING. Loop the free end of a ball of string round one end of the rump and tie a knot. Without cutting the string, make successive loops at 3 cm (1¼ inch) intervals along the rump; tighten each loop by pulling the string as you go. Secure the parcel by bringing the string under the entire length of the joint and knotting it to the free end.

Medallions of Veal with Green Peppercorns and Tomato Sauce

Serves 6
Working time: about 20 minutes
Total time: about 1 hour and 20 minutes (includes marinating)

Calories **150**
Protein **22g**
Cholesterol **90mg**
Total fat **6g**
Saturated fat **2g**
Sodium **180mg**

6	medallions of veal (about 125 g/4 oz each), trimmed of fat and neatly tied	6
1 tbsp	virgin olive oil	1 tbsp
1 tsp	dried green peppercorns, crushed	1 tsp
2 tbsp	brandy	2 tbsp
350 g	ripe tomatoes, skinned, seeded and chopped	12 oz
2 tsp	mixed dried herbs	2 tsp
1	garlic clove, crushed	1
¼ tsp	salt	¼ tsp
	freshly ground black pepper	
	watercress for garnish	

Mix the oil with the peppercorns in a shallow dish, add the medallions and turn them in the oil until they are evenly coated. Cover and allow to marinate at room temperature for at least 1 hour.

Heat a browning dish on high for the maximum time allowed in the instruction manual. Brown the medallions on both sides in the hot dish, then cover and microwave on high for 3 minutes, turning them over after 1½ minutes. Transfer the meat to a serving plate, cover with foil and set aside whilst making the sauce.

Stir the brandy into the browning dish and microwave on high for 1 minute, or until reduced by half.

Add the tomatoes, garlic, herbs, salt and pepper. Cover and microwave on high for 4 minutes, stirring frequently. Pour into a hot serving jug or bowl. Meanwhile, microwave the medallions on high for 1 minute more to heat through. Garnish with watercress and serve immediately with the tomato sauce.

SUGGESTED ACCOMPANIMENT: celery or bulb fennel hearts.

Medallions of Veal and Vegetables in Yogurt-Lemon Sauce

Serves 6
Working time: about 30 minutes
Total time: about 1 hour (includes marinating)

Calories **190**
Protein **24g**
Cholesterol **90mg**
Total fat **8g**
Saturated fat **2g**
Sodium **190mg**

6	medallions of veal (about 125 g/4 oz each), trimmed of fat and neatly tied	6
2 tbsp	virgin olive oil	2 tbsp
1	garlic clove, crushed	1
	freshly ground black pepper	
2	small onions, quartered	2
4	asparagus spears, trimmed and thinly sliced diagonally	4
125 g	button mushrooms, stems trimmed	4 oz
125 g	frozen peas	4 oz
15 g	flour	½ oz
1	lemon, finely grated rind only	1
¼ tsp	salt	¼ tsp
3 tbsp	plain low-fat yogurt	3 tbsp
	lemon wedges and parsley for garnish (optional)	

In a shallow dish, mix 1 tablespoon of the oil with the garlic and some pepper. Add the medallions and turn them in the oil until they are evenly coated. Cover and marinate at room temperature for at least 30 minutes.

About 15 minutes before cooking the medallions, put the remaining oil into a shallow dish and microwave on high for 30 seconds. Add the onions and asparagus, cover and microwave on high for 4 minutes, stirring after 2 minutes. Add the mushrooms and peas, cover and microwave on high for 6 minutes, stirring after 3 minutes. Meanwhile, in a small bowl, blend the flour with the lemon rind, salt, some pepper and the yogurt until smooth. Stir into the vegetables and microwave on high for 3 minutes, stirring after each minute. Remove from the microwave and keep warm whilst cooking the medallions.

Heat a browning dish on high for the maximum time allowed in the instruction manual. Brown both sides of the medallions in the hot dish. Cover and microwave on high for 1½ minutes, then turn the medallions over and microwave for a further 1 minute. Remove the meat to a hot serving dish, cover with foil and allow to stand for 1 minute.

Meanwhile, microwave the cooked vegetables on high for 1 minute to heat through. Serve the medallions, garnished with the lemon wedges and parsley, if using, accompanied by the hot vegetables.

Meatballs with Sweet Pepper Sauce

Serves 4
Working (and total) time: about 1 hour

Calories **280**
Protein **26g**
Cholesterol **90mg**
Total fat **12g**
Saturated fat **4g**
Sodium **385mg**

500 g	veal rump, trimmed of fat and very finely minced (page 15)	1 lb
90 g	brown breadcrumbs	3 oz
1	small onion, finely chopped	1
2 tbsp	chopped parsley	2 tbsp
1 tsp	mixed dried herbs	1 tsp
2 tbsp	virgin olive oil	2 tbsp
1	egg white	1
	freshly ground black pepper	
Red and green pepper sauce		
1	onion, thinly sliced	1
1	small sweet red pepper, thinly sliced	1
1	small sweet green pepper, thinly sliced	1
3	sticks celery, thinly sliced	3
2 tsp	paprika	2 tsp
2 tsp	tomato paste	2 tsp
30 cl	unsalted veal or chicken stock (recipes, page 138)	½ pint
¼ tsp	salt	¼ tsp

Place the veal in a large bowl with the brown breadcrumbs, chopped onion, parsley, mixed dried herbs, 1 tablespoon of the oil and the egg white. Season with freshly ground black pepper, then mix them all thoroughly together until smooth. Divide the mixture into 20 equal-sized pieces. With wet hands, roll each piece into a neat ball.

Heat a browning dish on high for the maximum time allowed in the instruction manual. Add the remaining oil to the dish. Put the meatballs into the oil and microwave on high, uncovered, for 5 to 6 minutes, turning and repositioning them every 2 minutes. Transfer them to a plate and set aside.

To make the sauce, add the sliced onion, sweet red and green peppers and celery to the oil remaining in the browning dish and stir. Microwave on high, uncovered, for 4 to 5 minutes, until the vegetables are softened. Stir in the paprika and microwave for 30 seconds. Stir in the tomato paste, stock and salt. Cover the dish and microwave on high for 8 minutes, stirring every 2 minutes.

Return the meatballs to the dish, coat them well with the sauce, then microwave on high for 2 minutes. Serve immediately.

SUGGESTED ACCOMPANIMENTS: *noodles; green salad.*

Making your own stock is easy enough, and the recipes that follow tell you how. Chicken or beef stock cubes may be substituted, but they are usually high in sodium; to counteract this, eliminate the salt from the recipe you are preparing.

Chicken Stock

Makes about 2 litres (3½ pints)
Working time: about 20 minutes
Total time: about 3 hours

2.5 kg	uncooked chicken trimmings and bones, bones cracked with a heavy knife	5 lb
2	carrots, cut into 1 cm (½ inch) thick rounds	2
2	sticks celery, cut into 2.5 cm (1 inch) pieces	2
2	large onions (about 500 g/1 lb) cut in half, one half stuck with 2 cloves	2
2	fresh thyme sprigs, or ½ tsp dried thyme	2
1 or 2	bay leaves	1 or 2
10 to 15	parsley stems	10 to 15
5	black peppercorns	5

Put the chicken trimmings and bones into a heavy stockpot; pour in enough water to cover them by about 5 cm (2 inches). Bring the liquid to the boil over medium heat, skimming off the scum that rises to the surface. Reduce the heat and simmer the liquid for 10 minutes, skimming and adding a little cold water to help precipitate the scum.

Add the vegetables, herbs and peppercorns, and submerge them in the liquid. If necessary, pour in enough additional water to cover the contents of the pot. Simmer the stock for 2 to 3 hours, skimming as necessary to remove the scum.

Strain the stock and discard the solids. Allow the stock to stand until it is tepid, then refrigerate it overnight to allow the fat to congeal. Spoon off and discard the layer of fat.

Tightly covered and refrigerated, the stock may be safely kept for 2 or 3 days. Stored in small, tightly covered freezer containers and frozen, the stock may be kept for as long as 6 months.

EDITOR'S NOTE: *The chicken gizzard and heart may be added to the stock. Wings and necks — rich in natural gelatine — produce a particularly gelatinous stock, ideal for sauces and jellied dishes. The liver should never be used for stock.*

Brown Stock

Makes about 3 litres (5 pints)
Working time: about 40 minutes
Total time: about 5½ hours

1.5 kg	veal breast (or veal or beef shin), cut into 7.5 cm (3 inch) pieces	3 lb
1.5 kg	uncooked veal or beef bones, cracked	3 lb
2	onions, quartered	2
2	sticks celery, chopped	2
2	carrots, sliced	2
3	unpeeled garlic cloves, crushed	3
8	black peppercorns	8
3	cloves	3
2 tsp	fresh thyme, or ½ tsp dried thyme	2 tsp
1	bay leaf	1

Preheat the oven to 220°C (425°F or Mark 7). Place the meat, bones, onions, celery and carrots in a large roasting pan and roast them in the oven until they are well browned — about 1 hour. Transfer them to a stockpot. Pour ½ litre (16 fl oz) of water into the roasting pan, scrape up the browned bits from the bottom and add the liquid to the pot.

Add the garlic, peppercorns and cloves. Add enough water to cover the contents by about 7.5 cm (3 inches). Bring to the boil, then reduce to a slow simmer, and skim any impurities from the surface. Add the thyme and bay leaf, then simmer very gently for 4 hours, skimming occasionally. Strain and discard the solids. Allow the stock to stand until it is tepid, then refrigerate it overnight. Spoon off and discard the layer of congealed fat.

Tightly covered and refrigerated, the stock may be safely kept for 2 or 3 days. Frozen, the stock may be kept for as long as 6 months.

EDITOR'S NOTE: *Browning in the oven should produce a rich mahogany colour. If your stock does not seem dark enough, cook 1 tablespoon of tomato paste in a small pan over medium heat, stirring constantly, until it darkens — about 3 minutes. Add this to the stock about 1 hour before the end of cooking. Any combination of meat and bones may be used. Ask your butcher to crack the bones.*

Veal Stock

For a light veal stock, follow the chicken stock recipe, but substitute 2.5 kg (5 lb) of veal bones for the chicken bones.

Glossary

Arrowroot: a tasteless, starchy, white powder, refined from the root of a tropical plant, that is used as a thickener. Unlike flour, it is transparent when cooked.

Balsamic vinegar: a mildly acid, intensely fragrant wine-based vinegar made in northern Italy. Traditionally it is aged in wooden casks.

Bâtonnet (also called bâton): a vegetable piece that has been cut in the shape of a stick — usually about 4 cm (1½ inches) long and 5 mm (¼ inch) square.

Bulb fennel: see Fennel.

Burghul (also called bulgur): whole-wheat kernels that have been steamed, dried and cracked.

Butterfly: to split a boneless cut of meat in half horizontally, leaving the halves hinged on one side.

Buttermilk: a tangy, cultured-milk product that, despite its name, contains about one third less fat than whole milk.

Calorie (or kilocalorie): a precise measure of the energy food supplies when it is broken down for use in the body.

Capers: the pickled flower buds of the caper plant, a shrub native to the Mediterranean. Capers should be rinsed before use to rid them of excess salt.

Caramelize: to heat sugar, or a naturally sugar-rich food such as onion, until the sugar becomes brown and syrupy.

Cardamom: the bittersweet, aromatic dried seeds or whole pods of a plant in the ginger family. Cardamom seeds may be used whole or ground.

Cayenne pepper: a fiery powder ground from the seeds and pods of various red chili peppers, used in small amounts to heighten other flavours.

Ceps (also called porcini): a variety of wild mushroom with a pungent, earthy flavour that survives drying or long cooking; they are often used in French and Italian cookery. Dried ceps should be soaked in hot water before use.

Chanterelle mushrooms: a variety of wild mushroom that is trumpet-shaped and yellow-orange in colour. Chanterelles are available fresh or dried; dried chanterelles should be soaked in hot water before use.

Chicory: a small, cigar-shaped vegetable, composed of many tightly wrapped white to pale-yellow leaves which have a pleasant bitter flavour.

Chiffonade: a leafy vegetable sliced into thin shreds.

Chili paste: a robust, spicy paste made of chili peppers, salt and other ingredients, among them garlic and black beans. Numerous kinds are available in Asian shops.

Chili peppers: a variety of hot red or green peppers. Serranos and jalapeños are small fresh green chilies that are extremely hot. Anchos are dried poblano chilies that are mildly hot and dark red in colour. Fresh or dried, chili peppers contain volatile oils that can irritate the skin and eyes; they must be handled with extreme care (caution, page 8). See also Chili paste.

Chinese cabbage: an elongated cabbage resembling cos lettuce, with long, broad ribs and crinkled, light-green to white leaves.

Chinese five-spice powder (also called five heavenly spices and five fragrant spices): a pungent blend of ground spices, most often fennel seeds, star anise, cloves, cinnamon or cassia, and Sichuan peppercorns; it should be used sparingly. If five-spice powder is unavailable, substitute a mixture of equal parts ground Sichuan peppercorns, cloves, cinnamon and fennel seeds.

Cholesterol: a wax-like substance that is manufactured in the human body and also found in foods of animal origin. Although a certain amount of cholesterol is necessary for proper body functioning, an excess can accumulate in the arteries, contributing to heart disease. See also Monounsaturated fats; Polyunsaturated fats; Saturated fats.

Coriander (also called cilantro): the pungent peppery leaves of the coriander plant or its earthy tasting dried seeds. It is a common seasoning in Middle-Eastern, Oriental and Latin-American cookery.

Cornflour: a starchy white powder made from corn kernels and used to thicken sauces. Like arrowroot, it is transparent when cooked and makes a more efficient thickener than flour. When cooked conventionally, a liquid containing cornflour must be stirred constantly in the early stages to prevent lumps from forming.

Cornichons: small, French, sour gherkin pickles.

Crystallized ginger (also called candied ginger): stems of young ginger preserved with sugar. Crystallized ginger should not be confused with ginger in syrup.

Cumin: the aromatic seeds of an umbelliferous plant similar to fennel used, whole or powdered, as a spice, especially in Indian and Latin-American dishes.

Daikon radish (also called mooli): a long, white Japanese radish.

Dark sesame oil: a seasoning oil, high in polyunsaturated fats, that is made from toasted sesame seeds. Because dark sesame oil has a relatively low smoking point, it is rarely used for sautéing. Dark sesame oil should not be confused or replaced with lighter sesame cooking oils.

Dijon mustard: a smooth or grainy mustard once manufactured only in Dijon, France; may be flavoured with herbs, green peppercorns or white wine.

Fennel: a herb (also called wild fennel) whose feathery leaves and dried seeds have a mild anise flavour. Its vegetable relative, the bulb — or Florence — fennel (also called finocchio) can be cooked, or eaten raw in salads.

Ginger: the spicy, buff-coloured, rootlike stem of the ginger plant, used as a seasoning either fresh or dried and powdered. The dried form should never be substituted for the fresh. See also Crystallized ginger.

Grand Marnier: a high-quality liqueur made from cognac and orange peel, which has a distinctive orange flavour.

Hoisin sauce: a thick, dark, reddish-brown sauce generally made from soya beans, flour, garlic, sugar and spices.

Julienne: to slice food into matchstick-sized pieces; also the name for the pieces themselves.

Juniper berries: the dried berries of the juniper tree, used as a key flavouring in gin as well as in meat marinades.

Madeira: a fortified wine from the island of Madeira. It has an underlying burnt flavour, which is the result of heating the wine after fermentation.

Mango: a fruit grown throughout the tropics, with sweet, succulent, yellow-orange flesh that is extremely rich in vitamin A. Like papaya, it may cause an allergic reaction in some individuals.

Marbling: the intramuscular fat that is found within meat. This fat cannot be trimmed away, but much of it can be rendered during cooking.

Marinade: a mixture of aromatic ingredients in which meat is allowed to stand before cooking to enrich its flavour. Some marinades will tenderize meat, but they do not penetrate deeply.

Marsala: a fortified dessert wine named after the region of Sicily where it originated. Most varieties are sweet in flavour and brown in colour.

Masa harina: a specially prepared corn flour used chiefly in the making of tortillas.

Meat thermometer: a thermometer that registers the internal temperature of a joint or steak in a matter of seconds.

Mirin: a sweet Japanese cooking wine that is made from rice. If mirin is unavailable, substitute white wine or sake mixed with a little sugar.

Monounsaturated fats: one of the three types of fats found in foods. Monounsaturated fats are believed not to raise the level of cholesterol in the blood.

Mozzarella: soft kneaded cheese from southern Italy, traditionally made from buffalo's milk, but now also made from cow's milk. Full-fat mozzarella has a fat content of 40 to 50 per cent, but lower-fat versions are available. The low-fat mozzarella used in the recipes in this book has a fat content of only about 16 per cent.

Olive oil: any of various grades of oil extracted from olives. Extra virgin olive oil has a full, fruity flavour and very low acidity. Virgin olive oil is lighter in flavour and slightly higher in acidity. Pure olive oil, a processed blend of olive oils, has the lightest taste and the highest acidity. To prevent rancidity, the oil should be stored in a cool, dark place.

Papaya (also called pawpaw): a tropical fruit, rich in vitamins A and C, whose juice contains the enzyme papain; the action of this enzyme breaks down the protein in meat and tenderizes it. Like mango, papaya may cause an allergic reaction in some individuals.

Persillade: a French term for chopped parsley mixed with garlic.

Phyllo (also spelt "filo"): a paper-thin flour-and-water pastry popular in Greece and the Middle East. It can be made at home or bought, fresh or frozen, from delicatessens and shops specializing in Middle-Eastern food. Because frozen phyllo dries out easily, it should be thawed in the refrigerator, and any phyllo sheets not in use should be covered with a damp towel.

Pine-nuts: seeds from the cone of the stone pine, a tree native to the Mediterranean. The buttery flavour of pine-nuts can be heightened by light toasting.

Polyunsaturated fats: one of the three types of fats found in foods. They exist in abundance in such vegetable oils as safflower, sunflower, corn or soya bean. Polyunsaturated fats lower the level of cholesterol in the blood.

Port: a sweet fortified wine originally produced in northern Portugal and shipped through the city of Oporto.

Pot roast: a chunky piece of beef cooked by braising.

Prosciutto: an uncooked, dry-cured and slightly salty

Italian ham that is sliced paper-thin before serving.

Quark: a type of soft cheese with a mild, clean, slightly acid flavour; usually low in fat, but smoother varieties have added cream.

Recommended Daily Amount (RDA): the average daily amount of an essential nutrient recommended for healthy people by the U.K. Department of Health and Social Security.

Reduce: to boil down a liquid or sauce in order to concentrate its flavour or thicken its consistency.

Rice vinegar: a mild, fragrant vinegar that is less assertive than cider vinegar or distilled white vinegar. It is available in dark, light, seasoned and sweetened varieties; Japanese rice vinegar generally is milder than the Chinese version.

Rind: the flavourful outermost layer of citrus-fruit peel; it should be cut or grated free of the white pith that lies just beneath it.

Safflower oil: a vegetable oil that contains the highest proportion of polyunsaturated fats.

Saffron: the dried, yellowish-red stigmas, or threads, of the saffron crocus (*Crocus sativus*); saffron yields a pungent flavour and a brilliant yellow colour. Powdered saffron may be substituted for the threads but has less flavour.

Saturated fats: one of the three types of fats found in food. They exist in abundance in animal products and coconut and palm oils; they raise the level of cholesterol in the blood. Because high blood-cholesterol levels may cause heart disease, saturated fat consumption should be restricted to less than 15 per cent of the calories provided by the daily diet.

Scaloppini: cutlets sliced or pounded thin.

Sear: to brown the surface of meat by a short application of intense heat; searing adds flavour as well as colour.

Sesame oil: see Dark sesame oil.

Shallot: a mild variety of onion, with a subtle flavour and papery, red-brown skin. If shallots are unavailable, substitute spring onions in a recipe.

Shiitake mushrooms: a variety of mushroom, originally cultivated only in Japan, that is sold fresh or dried. The dried version should be stored in a cool, dry place; it may be reconstituted by 20 to 30 minutes' soaking in water before use.

Sodium: a nutrient essential to maintaining the proper balance of fluids in the body. In most diets, a major source of the element is table salt, which contains 40 per cent sodium. Excess sodium may contribute to high blood pressure, which increases the risk of heart disease. One teaspoon (5.5 g) of salt, with 2,132 milligrams of sodium, contains just over the maximum daily amount recommended by the World Health Organization.

Soy sauce: a savoury, salty brown liquid made from fermented soya beans. One tablespoon of ordinary soy sauce contains about 1,030 milligrams of sodium; lower-sodium variations, as used in the recipes in this book, may contain as little as half that amount.

Stir-fry: to cook thin pieces of meat or vegetables, or a combination of both, over high heat in a small amount of oil, stirring constantly to ensure even cooking in a short time. The traditional cooking vessel is a Chinese wok; a large, non-stick or heavy frying pan may also be used for stir-frying.

Stock: a savoury broth that is made by simmering aromatic vegetables, herbs, spices, bones and meat trimmings in water. Stock is often used as a flavour-rich liquid for braising meat and making sauces.

Sun-dried tomatoes: tomatoes that have been naturally dried in the sun, to concentrate their flavour and preserve them; some are then packed in oil with seasoning and herbs.

Sweet chili sauce: any of a group of Asian sauces containing chili peppers, vinegar, garlic, sugar and salt. The sauce may be used as a condiment to accompany meats, poultry or fish, or it may be included as an ingredient in a dish. When sweet chili sauce is unavailable, make it at home by mixing 1 tablespoon each of golden syrup and rice vinegar with 1 to 2 teaspoons of crushed hot red pepper flakes.

Tarragon: a strong herb with a sweet anise taste. In combination with other herbs — especially rosemary, sage or thyme — it should be used sparingly, to avoid a clash of flavours. Because heat intensifies tarragon's flavour, cooked dishes require smaller amounts.

Tenderize: to make meat tender by pounding, grinding, or slow cooking in moist heat — or by the use of a substance containing enzymes that break down meat protein.

Tofu (also called bean curd): a dense, unfermented soya bean product with a mild flavour. It is rich in protein, relatively low in calories and free of cholesterol. Lightly pressed silken tofu is used for blending into other ingredients; heavily pressed firm tofu, which has a texture similar to cheese, may be cubed or sliced. Soft tofu, with a texture midway between the two, is also available.

Tomato paste: a concentrated tomato purée, available in cans and tubes, used in sauces and soups.

Turmeric: a spice used as a colouring agent and occasionally as a substitute for saffron. It has a musty odour and a slightly bitter flavour.

Udon: a fine, flat Japanese wheat noodle.

Vine leaves: the tender, delicately flavoured leaves of the grapevine. Vine leaves are used in many Mediterranean cuisines as wrappers for savoury fillings. Fresh vine leaves should be cooked for 5 minutes in boiling water before they are used in a recipe; vine leaves packed in brine should be thoroughly rinsed.

Wheat berries (also called whole wheat grain): unpolished, whole wheat kernels with a nutty taste and a chewy texture.

Wild rice: the seed of a water grass native to the Great Lakes region of North America. Wild rice is appreciated for its robust flavour.

Index

Picture Credits

Cover: James Murphy. 4: top, Michael Latil; bottom left, Renée Comet; bottom right, James Murphy. 5: top, James Murphy; bottom, Michael Latil. 6: James Murphy. 10: James Murphy. 12-14: Renée Comet. 15: James Murphy. 16: top, Michael Latil; bottom, Renée Comet. 17: Lisa Masson. 18: Steven Biver. 19: top, Taran Z; bottom, Michael Latil. 20-23: Renée Comet. 24: Michael Latil. 25: Taran Z. 26-27: Renée Comet. 28: Steven Biver. 29-31: Tom Belshaw. 32: James Murphy. 33: Chris Knaggs. 34-36: Tom Belshaw. 37: Lisa Masson. 38: Chris Knaggs. 39: Rachel Andrew.

40: Renée Comet. 41: Michael Latil. 42-44: Renée Comet. 45: Steven Biver. 46-47: Renée Comet. 48: Lisa Masson. 49-51: Renée Comet. 52: Michael Latil. 53: Taran Z. 54-59: Tom Belshaw. 60: James Murphy. 62-67: Renée Comet. 68: Tom Belshaw. 69: James Murphy. 70: top, Michael Latil; bottom Taran Z. 71: Steven Biver. 72-73: Renée Comet. 74: Tom Belshaw. 75-78: Chris Knaggs. 79-82: James Murphy. 83: Rachel Andrew. 84: Renée Comet. 85: Steven Biver. 86-92: Renée Comet. 93: James Murphy. 94: Rachel Andrew. 95: James Murphy. 96: Chris Knaggs. 97-99: Renée

Comet. 100-104: James Murphy. 105: Chris Knaggs. 106-107: James Murphy. 108: Chris Knaggs. 110: James Murphy. 111: Renée Comet. 112: top, Michael Latil; bottom, Renée Comet. 113: Renée Comet. 114: Taran Z. 115: Renée Comet. 116: Taran Z. 117: Michael Latil. 118: James Murphy. 119: Chris Knaggs. 121-122: James Murphy. 123: Chris Knaggs. 124: James Murphy. 125: Chris Knaggs. 126: Michael Latil. 128-129: Renée Comet. 130-131: Michael Latil. 132-134: Chris Knaggs. 135: top, James Murphy; bottom, Chris Knaggs. 136-137: Chris Knaggs.

Acknowledgements

The editors are particularly indebted to the following people for creating recipes for this volume: Melanie Barnard, New Canaan, Ct.; Peter Brett, Washington, D.C.; Nora Carey, Paris; Robert Chambers, New York; Brooke Dojny, Westport, Ct.; Marie Lou, Bethesda, Md.; Jenni Wright, London.

The editors also wish to thank: Moira Banks, London; Alison Birch, London; Mary Jane Blandford, Alexandria, Va., U.S.A.; Joe Booker, Zamoiski Co., Baltimore, Md., U.S.A.; Jo Calabrese, Royal Worcester Spode Inc., New York; Alexandra Carlier, London; Jackie Chalkley, Washington, D.C.; La Cuisine, Alexandria, Va., U.S.A.; Jeanne Dale, The Pilgrim Glass Corp., New York; Rex Downey, Oxon Hill, Md., U.S.A.; Flowers Unique, Alexandria, Va., U.S.A.; Dennis Garrett and Ed Nash, The American Hand Plus, Washington, D.C.; Judith Goodkind, Alexandria, Va., U.S.A.; Carol Gvozdich, Alexandria, Va., U.S.A.; Chong Su Han, Grass Roots Restaurant, Alexandria, Va., U.S.A.; Jane Hawker, London; Elizabeth Hodgson, London; Kitchen Bazaar, Washington, D.C.; KitchenAid, Inc., Troy, Ohio, U.S.A.; Rebecca Johns, Alexandria, Va., U.S.A.; Gary Latzman and Kirk Phillips, Retroneu, New York; Nancy Lendved, Alexandria, Va., U.S.A.; Leon, Stanley, Evan and Mark Lobel, New York; Magruder's, Inc., Rockville, Md.; Nambé Mills Inc., Sante Fe, N. Mex., U.S.A.; Robin Olsen, London; Oster, Milwaukee, Wis., U.S.A.; Lisa Ownby, Alexandria, Va., U.S.A.; Prabhu Ponkshe, American Heart Association, Washington, D.C.; C. Kyle and Ruth Randall, Alexandria, Va., U.S.A.; Linda Robertson, JUD Tile, Vienna, Va., U.S.A.; Schiller & Asmus, Inc., Yemasse, S.C., U.S.A.; Jeanette Smyth, Alexandria, Va., U.S.A.; Straight from the Crate, Inc., Alexandria, Va., U.S.A.; Anne Steiner, Alexandria, Va., U.S.A.; Paula Sussman, Alexandria, Va., U.S.A.; Ann Vaughan, Jenn-Air Company, Indianapolis, Ind., U.S.A.; Rita Walters, London; Sarah Wiley, London; Williams-Sonoma, Inc., Alexandria, Va., and Washington, D.C.; CiCi Williamson, Alexandria, Va., U.S.A.; Lynn Addison Yorke, Cheverly, Md., U.S.A.

Typesetting by G. Beard and Son Ltd., Brighton, Sussex, England
Printed in Italy by New Interlitho S.p.A. - Milan